T0049607

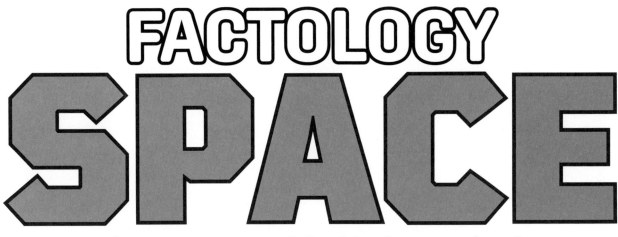

FACTOLOGY
SPACE

Open up a world of information!

ARE YOU READY
TO EXPLORE...

Standby to unlock the greatest secrets of our solar system... and what lies beyond it! For thousands of years, humans have wondered what's really going on in the night sky. The answers are more incredible than we could ever have imagined – even after giant leaps of discovery, there's so much more for us to explore! As mankind gets set to boldly go further than ever before, hop on board and take a journey through the cosmos.

Want to know what it's really like to be an astronaut? The drive to survive (and thrive) in space has changed the way we live – from the clothes we wear to the ways we work together. Learn what it takes to make it in space... it all starts with a few bright ideas! From astronomers to astronauts, incredible people have proven that thinking big hasn't only transformed the way we see worlds beyond ours, but also the one we currently call home, too.

SPACE

3.2.1...
BLAST OFF

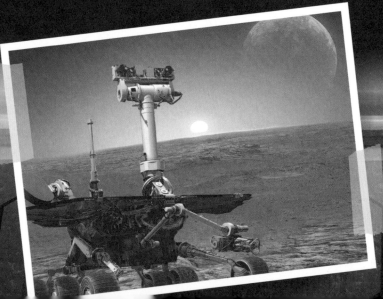

CHAPTER 1

OUR INCREDIBLE UNIVERSE

From gas giants to dwarf planets, baby stars to supermassive black holes and meteorites to the Milky Way, our universe is an amazing place filled with mind-blowing stuff! Read on for a light-speed tour of the Big Bang, our remarkable solar system and beyond...

THE **BIG** BANG

Our universe hasn't been around forever. Both space and time started in a cataclysmic event 13.8 billion years ago that astronomers call the Big Bang

0 YEARS

TIME BEGINS

1 TRILLION°C

0.32 SECONDS

1 SECOND

100 SECONDS

1 YEAR

100 YEARS

STARTS TO COOL

380,000 YEARS

The observable universe is thought to be **93 BILLION LIGHT YEARS** in diameter – and still expanding!

THE FIRST STARS

100 MILLION YEARS

1 BILLION YEARS

Cosmic microwave background

To begin with, the new universe was filled only with energy, but over time some of that energy was turned into atoms.

For the first 380,000 years, there was so much stuff flying around inside the new universe that light couldn't escape. Whenever it tried, it bumped into something and was knocked off course. After a long time, the universe cooled enough and the light was let out all at once – astronomers call it the Cosmic Microwave Background.

FIRST STARS AND GALAXIES

After a hundred million years or so, gravity drew some of the universe's atoms together to make the first stars. Those stars gathered into groups called galaxies. Astronomers estimate there are now two trillion galaxies in the universe, including ours – a beautiful spiral galaxy called the Milky Way.

OUR SOLAR SYSTEM

A gas cloud within the Milky Way collapsed around 4.6 billion years ago, setting off a chain of events that ignited the Sun. However, not all the atoms in that cloud made it into the Sun. Some were left in a flat disc around it that gravity slowly turned into the planets.

There are stars so far away that their light hasn't reached Earth!

Astronomers think a mysterious force that repels gravity called dark energy is speeding up the expansion of the universe.

Meanwhile, a strange invisible 'glue' called

DARK MATTER

is holding galaxies together.

OUR SOLAR SYSTEM

THE MILKY WAY

The Milky Way belongs to a group of galaxies called The Local Group.

You are made of stardust

The Sun wasn't the first star those atoms had been part of! An earlier star had exploded and blasted its atoms across the galaxy. Some of those atoms are now in the Sun, some are in the Earth and some are in you!

GALAXY CLUSTERS

10 BILLION YEARS

Not all galaxies are spirals – ellipticals are shaped like rugby balls and lenticulars like cigars.

THE SUN

MERCURY

VENUS

ICE LINE

MARS

EARTH

Astronomers have found nearly a
million asteroids in the Asteroid Belt!
A fifth rocky planet would have formed
out of the material in the Asteroid Belt
were it not for the gravity of Jupiter.
The giant planet prevents these lumps
of rock and metal left over from the
formation of the solar system from
sticking together.

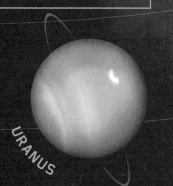

JUPITER

A group of asteroids known as
the TROJANS share Jupiter's orbit.

The giant planets probably didn't start out
where they are today. Astronomers think
that Jupiter has moved inwards and the
other three giant planets headed further
from the Sun. It's even possible that Uranus
and Neptune swapped order. We're lucky
Jupiter stopped, otherwise it might have
knocked into the Earth!

URANUS

The planets' orbits are not circles. They are oval-shaped 'ellipses'.

The KUIPER BELT is a band of
small objects orbiting the Sun
beyond Neptune.

SUN	MERCURY	EARTH		JUPITER	SATURN
	VENUS		MARS		
	0.4 AU	0.7 AU	1 AU	1.5 AU	5.2 AU	9.5 AU

OUR SOLAR SYSTEM

SATURN

Our solar system has eight planets orbiting around the only star in the system, the Sun. There are also hundreds of satellites orbiting planets, as well as asteroids, dwarf planets and many other bodies, mostly in the Asteroid Belt and the faraway Kuiper Belt

Temperatures in the early solar system were so high close to the Sun that everything but rock and metal was boiled away. That's why the inner four rocky planets – Mercury, Venus, Earth and Mars – are all small and solid. Earth's water and atmosphere were added later through volcanic eruptions and asteroid impacts from space.

NEPTUNE

Beyond a place called the 'ice line', temperatures were a lot cooler. Some liquids and gases froze solid and gas gathered around them to make the giant planets. Jupiter and Saturn are 'gas giants'. Uranus and Neptune are 'ice giants'. Together, this large quartet are over 200 times heavier than the rocky planets.

Astronomers are starting to believe that there's a ninth planet in the solar system. They have seen small objects journeying around the Sun further out than the Kuiper Belt. Their orbits are all lined up, suggesting something is herding them into these positions.

THIS 'PLANET NINE' WOULD BE BIGGER THAN EARTH!

URANUS   As you can see here, the planets are not equally spaced out.   NEPTUNE

19 AU   30 AU

AU - ASTRONOMICAL UNIT (1 AU = 150 MILLION KM)

OUR SOLAR SYSTEM

Ancient people connected the stars to draw patterns called **CONSTELLATIONS**

GEOCENTRIC SOLAR SYSTEM

EARTH

Our early ancestors believed that the Sun, Moon and the planets all moved around the Earth. This made sense because it doesn't feel like the Earth is moving.

Astronomers call this a 'geocentric' model, meaning a central Earth. It's an idea that remained popular for more than a thousand years!

Everything changed when we invented the telescope in the 1600s – a device that allows us to see further and take a closer look at objects in space.

GALILEO GALILEI
(1564–1642)

CRATERS ON
THE MOON

THE PHASES
OF VENUS

THE MOONS
OF JUPITER

Looking at Jupiter and Venus, an Italian astronomer called Galileo found evidence that made it clear the Earth orbits a central Sun (a 'heliocentric' model). Venus has phases like the Moon – impossible if it orbits the Earth.

HELIOCENTRIC SOLAR SYSTEM

SUN

In the late 1600s, English scientist Isaac Newton discovered why the planets orbit the Sun – a force called gravity. He saw an apple fall to the ground and realised that the same force pulling the apple down was pulling the planets in giant loops around the Sun.

FAST

A famous story says the apple hit Newton on the head, but it didn't!

FACT

Now we know that our Sun is just one star out of trillions and trillions in the universe.

TODAY, ASTRONOMERS HAVE BEEN ABLE TO FIND OUT A LOT MORE INFORMATION

The Sun is 150 million km (or 1 Astronomical Unit) away from Earth.

12 ASTRONAUTS left their footprints on the Moon between **1969** and **1972**

We know that the Sun is made of hydrogen and helium.

Soon we might **SEND PEOPLE TO MARS** for the first time.

WE ALSO KNOW MORE ABOUT THE PLANETS THAN EVER BEFORE

We have sent special machines to explore all eight planets, as well as some of the asteroids, comets, moons and dwarf planets that make up the Sun's family of orbiting worlds.

Our Sun is a colossal energy factory constantly churning hydrogen into helium deep in its core. This process creates sunlight, which takes more than 100,000 years to make its way through the Sun's layers to reach the surface. From there it takes around eight minutes to reach the Earth

AROUND THE JOURNEY

YOU COULD FIT MORE THAN **1.3 MILLION EARTHS** INSIDE THE SUN (OR 1,000 JUPITERS)

4,370,005.6KM ROUND
AT THE EQUATOR

Solar storms

The Sun burps out massive storms into the solar system known as coronal mass ejections. A billion tonnes of material can be spat out at over 1.5 million kilometres per hour. They flood the solar system with electrically charged particles that trigger aurorae (northern and southern lights) when they reach the planets.

THE LIFE CYCLE OF THE SUN

MOST STARS ARE SMALLER THAN THE SUN **ALTHOUGH SOME ARE MUCH LARGER**

SUN

RED GIANT

PLANETARY NEBULA

WHITE DWARF

BLACK DWARF

ASTRONOMERS CALL THE SUN A **G2V YELLOW DWARF STAR**

YOU SHOULD **NEVER** LOOK AT THE SUN WITHOUT PROTECTIVE EQUIPMENT

SUN

A stream of particles called **THE SOLAR WIND** blows outwards from the Sun.

Sunspots

Dark blemishes are often seen on the surface of the Sun. Astronomers call them sunspots. They are simply cooler regions where really intense magnetic activity keeps some heat from reaching the surface of the Sun. Often appearing in pairs, they are regularly bigger than the Earth.

The Moon is the brightest object in the night sky because it's the closest thing to us in space. It doesn't make any light of its own, instead it reflects light from the Sun like a mirror. How much light it reflects towards us depends on its position around the Earth.

DAY LENGTH	27.3 Earth days
YEAR LENGTH	27.3 Earth days
GRAVITY	0.17 of Earth's
AVERAGE TEMPERATURE	−53°C
DISTANCE FROM EARTH	384,400km

6.68°
AXIS

10,917KM ROUND
AT THE EQUATOR

Two tortoises flew around the Moon as part of the Soviet Union's 1968 Zond 5 mission.

All the other planets would fit in the gap between the Earth and the Moon.

384,400KM

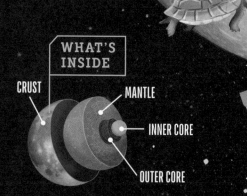

WHAT'S INSIDE

CRUST

MANTLE

INNER CORE

OUTER CORE

THE MOON
IS MOVING AWAY FROM
THE EARTH
BY
3.8cm EVERY YEAR

Making the Moon

Astronomers believe the Moon was formed from the Earth. When our planet was still very young it was hit by a planet the size of Mars. The calamitous collision sent a lot of debris flying into orbit around the Earth. Gravity collected it together to form the Moon.

Lunar phases

As the Moon goes around the Earth, it waxes and wanes through a series of phases from a new Moon to a full Moon and back again. Waxing means growing and waning means shrinking. If the Moon is more than half full, it is called gibbous.

THE MOON TAKES
27.3 DAYS
TO ORBIT THE EARTH YET FULL MOONS OCCUR EVERY
29.5 DAYS

That's because a full Moon happens when the Sun, Earth and Moon are all in a line. It takes the Moon a couple of days to catch up with the fact we've moved around the Sun while it was orbiting us. We only ever see one side of the Moon from the Earth, never the far side.

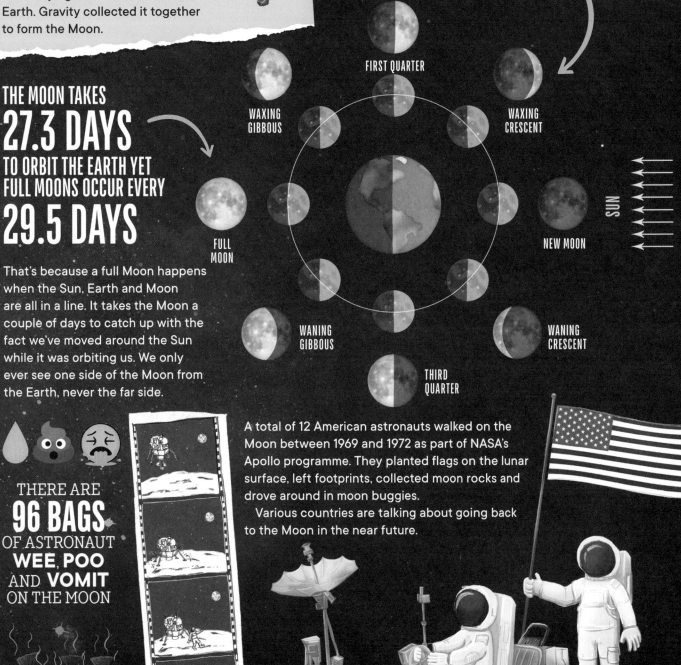

FIRST QUARTER

WAXING GIBBOUS

WAXING CRESCENT

FULL MOON

NEW MOON

SUN

WANING GIBBOUS

WANING CRESCENT

THIRD QUARTER

THERE ARE
96 BAGS
OF ASTRONAUT WEE, POO AND VOMIT ON THE MOON

A total of 12 American astronauts walked on the Moon between 1969 and 1972 as part of NASA's Apollo programme. They planted flags on the lunar surface, left footprints, collected moon rocks and drove around in moon buggies.

Various countries are talking about going back to the Moon in the near future.

PLANET POWER

There are eight planets in our solar system and all of them orbit the Sun. From the sweltering surface of Mercury to the eerie blue light of Uranus, find out more about Earth's galactic neighbourhood...

MERCURY

· FAST ·
There are records of humans observing Mercury as early as **3,500 YEARS AGO**
· FACT ·

DAY LENGTH	58. 65 Earth days
YEAR LENGTH	87.97 Earth days
GRAVITY	0.4 of Earth's
TEMPERATURE	430°C to -180°C
DISTANCE FROM SUN	0.4 AU
MOONS	0

2°
AXIS

15,329KM ROUND
AT THE EQUATOR

MESSENGER
The planet is so close to the Sun, feeling such extreme gravity, that it has probably never had a moon of its own. Instead, the only thing ever to orbit Mercury is the human-made MESSENGER space probe sent by NASA to explore the planet between 2011 and 2015.

MESSENGER
SPACE PROBE

Just a little bit larger than Earth's moon, Mercury is the smallest planet in the solar system as well as the closest to the Sun. Its day side is baked to 430°C but, without a thick atmosphere to hold in the heat, night-time temperatures plummet to -180°C.

CRUST   MANTLE

WHAT'S INSIDE?

SOLID INNER CORE

LIQUID OUTER CORE

DISTANCE FROM SUN

0.4 AU
AU - ASTRONOMICAL UNIT (1 AU = 150 MILLION KM)

26
Fe
IRON

The planet's core contains more iron than any other planet.

VENUS

NAMED AFTER THE
ROMAN GODDESS
OF
LOVE & BEAUTY

DAY LENGTH	243 Earth days
YEAR LENGTH	225 Earth days
GRAVITY	0.91 of Earth's
MAXIMUM TEMPERATURE	480°C
DISTANCE FROM SUN	0.7 AU
MOONS	0

177.3°
AXIS

38,025KM ROUND
AT THE EQUATOR

ONLY PLANET TO
SPIN CLOCKWISE

VENERA 7

Evil twin

Sometimes Venus is called 'Earth's twin', but the only similarity is size. Our nearest planetary neighbour is a hellish world with thick carbon dioxide clouds crushing down onto the surface. Not only can temperatures reach 465°C, the air is laced with burning sulphuric acid. You'd be baked, crushed and dissolved.

Despite its unfriendly conditions, we have landed some probes onto Venus's surface. The first – the Soviet Union's Venera 7 in 1970 – managed to hold out for 23 minutes before succumbing to the horrible climate.

More recently, the Venus Express and Akatsuki probes have studied the planet from orbit.

WHAT'S INSIDE

CRUST

METALLIC INNER CORE

ROCKY MANTLE

0.7 AU

VENUS EXPRESS

▶ Radio waves are used to read the surface of Venus at a safe distance

MADE TO ORDER

The size and order of the planets is a result of the way our solar system formed. The first four are small, with rocky surfaces. Beyond them are the gas and ice giants, and even further out lies the Kuiper Belt, home to the dwarf planet Pluto.

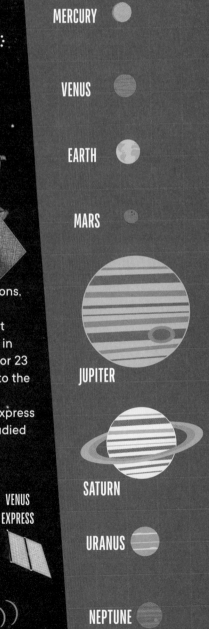

MERCURY

VENUS

EARTH

MARS

JUPITER

SATURN

URANUS

NEPTUNE

Our planet is the only one known to host life. We have
plenty of liquid water – a crucial ingredient for living things
– because we sit in the perfect warm spot around the Sun.
Astronomers call it the Goldilocks Zone after the porridge
in the fairytale. Not too hot, not too cold – just right!

EARTH

IF EARTH
WERE AN APPLE
THE CRUST
WOULD ONLY BE
AS THICK AS
THE SKIN

EXOSPHERE 690KM
THERMOSPHERE 600KM
KÁRMÁN LINE 100KM
MESOSPHERE 85KM
STRATOSPHERE 50KM
TROPOSPHERE 20KM

23.4⁰
AXIS

40,075KM ROUND
AT THE EQUATOR

WHAT'S
INSIDE

CRUST MANTLE

SOLID
INNER
CORE

LIQUID
OUTER
CORE

DAY LENGTH	24 hours
YEAR LENGTH	365 days
GRAVITY	9.81m/s²
AVERAGE TEMPERATURE	15°C
DISTANCE FROM SUN	1 AU
MOONS	1

1 AU

The Moon plays a big part in the tides. Together with the Sun, it
pulls on the Earth and creates a bulge of water on one side of
our planet – an area of high tide. The water is pulled away from
the top and bottom of the Earth, creating areas of low tide.

Oh, what an atmosphere!

The atmosphere above our heads is 78% nitrogen and 21% oxygen, with the other 1% made of small traces of other gases such as carbon dioxide. We need the oxygen to breathe, and the sky is constantly being reflled with it by plants, trees and microbes in the ocean.

THE MOON IS 384,400KM AWAY FROM THE EARTH THAT'S THE DISTANCE OF AROUND 30 EARTHS

The seasons

We experience changing seasons because the Earth's axis is tilted. It's summer when our half of the planet is tilted towards the Sun. Winter comes when we're tipped away. We have the gravity of the Moon to thank for the angle of our axis staying the same. Otherwise the seasons would change wildly.

LOW TIDE

HIGH TIDE

HIGH TIDE

LOW TIDE

71% OF THE EARTH'S SURFACE IS COVERED IN WATER

DAY LENGTH	24 hrs 37 mins
YEAR LENGTH	687 Earth days
GRAVITY	0.38 of Earth's
AVERAGE TEMPERATURE	–60°C
DISTANCE FROM SUN	1.5 AU
MOONS	2

25°
AXIS

21,344KM ROUND
AT THE EQUATOR

MARS IS RED BECAUSE THE IRON IN ITS ROCKS HAS TURNED TO RUST

WHAT'S INSIDE

CRUST

MANTLE

INNER CORE

Mars has two moons – Phobos and Deimos. Both are very small, just tens of kilometres across. That's the size of a city. Phobos is gradually spiralling inwards and, in around 30 million years' time, Mars's gravity will rip it into pieces to form a ring around the Red Planet.

PHOBOS
22KM DIAMETER

9,378KM

DEIMOS
12KM DIAMETER

23,460KM

1.5 AU

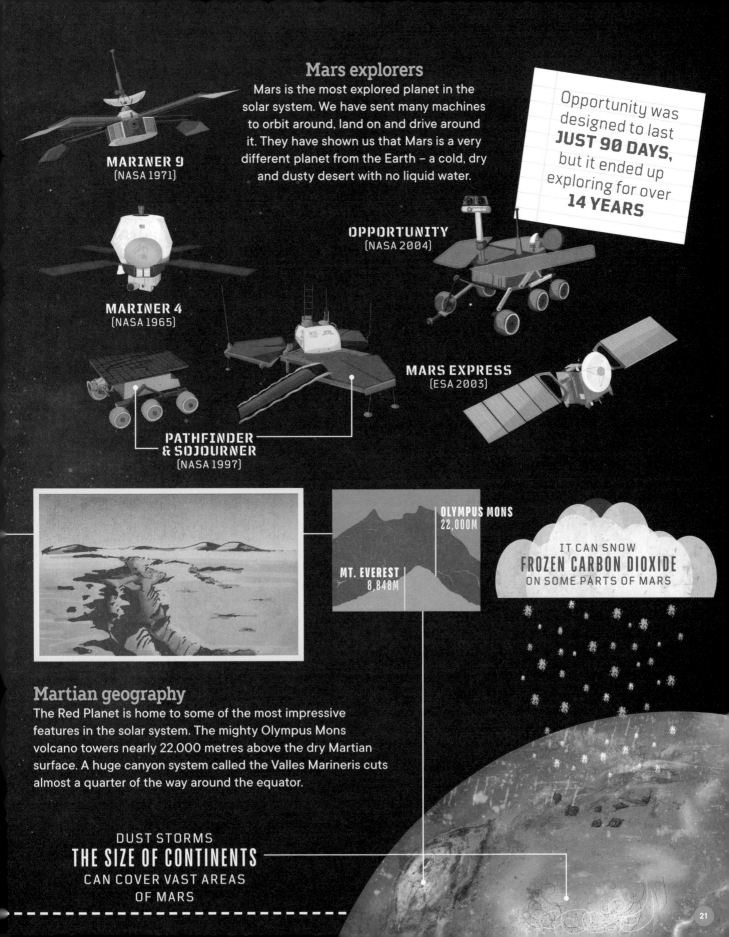

Mars explorers

Mars is the most explored planet in the solar system. We have sent many machines to orbit around, land on and drive around it. They have shown us that Mars is a very different planet from the Earth – a cold, dry and dusty desert with no liquid water.

MARINER 9
(NASA 1971)

MARINER 4
(NASA 1965)

OPPORTUNITY
(NASA 2004)

Opportunity was designed to last **JUST 90 DAYS,** but it ended up exploring for over **14 YEARS**

PATHFINDER & SOJOURNER
(NASA 1997)

MARS EXPRESS
(ESA 2003)

OLYMPUS MONS
22,000M

MT. EVEREST
8,848M

IT CAN SNOW
FROZEN CARBON DIOXIDE
ON SOME PARTS OF MARS

Martian geography

The Red Planet is home to some of the most impressive features in the solar system. The mighty Olympus Mons volcano towers nearly 22,000 metres above the dry Martian surface. A huge canyon system called the Valles Marineris cuts almost a quarter of the way around the equator.

DUST STORMS
THE SIZE OF CONTINENTS
CAN COVER VAST AREAS
OF MARS

JUPITER

WHAT'S INSIDE

HYDROGEN ATMOSPHERE

LIQUID HYDROGEN

ICE AND ROCK INNER CORE

METALLIC HYDROGEN

3.1° AXIS

439,264KM ROUND AT THE EQUATOR

Even through a small telescope you'll see Jupiter's surface is split into different coloured bands called 'equatorial belts'. Hidden in these stripes are huge storms where winds can rage at 644 kilometres per hour. It is also noticeably fatter at the equator because it bulges outwards as it spins.

JUNO SATELLITE

NASA'S JUNO MISSION CARRIED 3 ALUMINIUM LEGO FIGURES TO JUPITER

The biggest storm on Jupiter is called 'The Great Red Spot', although it's not as great as it used to be. At one point you could fit four Earths inside! Now it's more like two and a half. Astronomers are still trying to figure out why it's shrinking.

DAY LENGTH	9 hrs 50 mins
YEAR LENGTH	11.86 Earth years
GRAVITY	2.52 of Earth's
AVERAGE TEMPERATURE	–150°C
DISTANCE FROM SUN	5.2 AU
MOONS	80+

Jupiter has some of the most interesting moons in the solar system. IO looks like a giant, mouldy pizza because volcanoes are constantly spewing sulphur onto the surface. Its neighbour, Europa, has a huge ocean of water hidden under vast sheets of ice. Ganymede is the biggest moon in the solar system.

GANYMEDE 5,268KM DIAMETER

CALLISTO 4,821KM DIAMETER

IO 3,643KM DIAMETER

EUROPA 3,121KM DIAMETER

Jupiter has the shortest day of any planet – just 9 hours and 50 minutes

You could fit all of the other planets inside Jupiter!

5.2 AU

Saturn has some of the most impressive moons in the solar system. Its largest – Titan – is bigger than the planet Mercury and is the only satellite in the solar system with a thick atmosphere. Space scientists landed the Huygens Probe on its icy surface in January 2005.

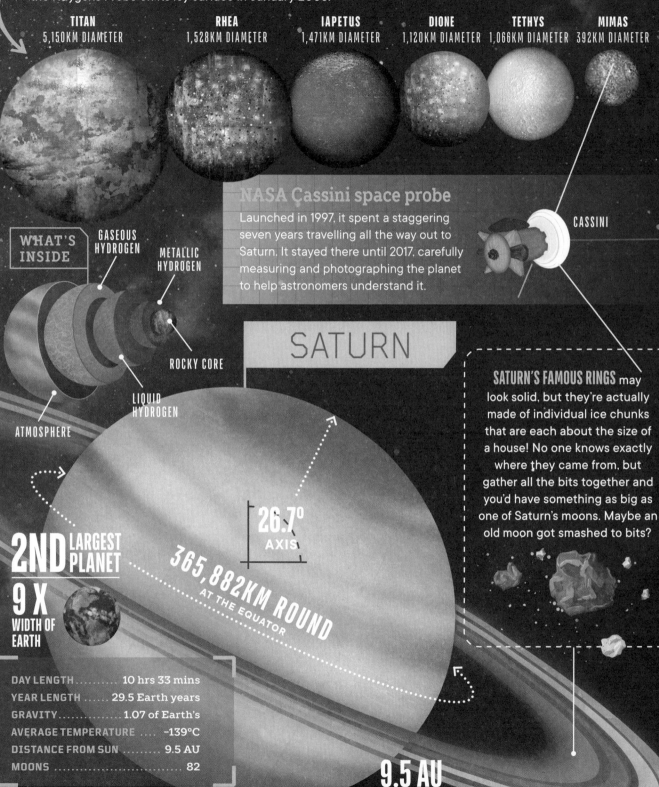

TITAN
5,150KM DIAMETER

RHEA
1,528KM DIAMETER

IAPETUS
1,471KM DIAMETER

DIONE
1,120KM DIAMETER

TETHYS
1,066KM DIAMETER

MIMAS
392KM DIAMETER

NASA Cassini space probe

Launched in 1997, it spent a staggering seven years travelling all the way out to Saturn. It stayed there until 2017, carefully measuring and photographing the planet to help astronomers understand it.

CASSINI

WHAT'S INSIDE

GASEOUS HYDROGEN

METALLIC HYDROGEN

ROCKY CORE

LIQUID HYDROGEN

ATMOSPHERE

SATURN

SATURN'S FAMOUS RINGS may look solid, but they're actually made of individual ice chunks that are each about the size of a house! No one knows exactly where they came from, but gather all the bits together and you'd have something as big as one of Saturn's moons. Maybe an old moon got smashed to bits?

26.7°
AXIS

2ND LARGEST PLANET

9 X WIDTH OF EARTH

365,882KM ROUND AT THE EQUATOR

DAY LENGTH	10 hrs 33 mins
YEAR LENGTH	29.5 Earth years
GRAVITY	1.07 of Earth's
AVERAGE TEMPERATURE	-139°C
DISTANCE FROM SUN	9.5 AU
MOONS	82

9.5 AU

URANUS

WHAT'S INSIDE

GAS ATMOSPHERE

MOLTEN ROCK CORE

ICY WATER, METHANE AND AMMONIA

LIQUID HYDROGEN

DAY LENGTH	17 hrs 14 mins
YEAR LENGTH	84 Earth years
GRAVITY	0.89 of Earth's
AVERAGE TEMPERATURE	–195°C
DISTANCE FROM SUN	19 AU
MOONS	27

159,354KM ROUND AT THE EQUATOR

97.8° AXIS

URANUS HAS **13** RINGS

The seventh planet orbits the Sun on its side – its axis is tipped over by more than ninety degrees. That means that for half of Uranus's 84-year orbit, one pole is constantly in the dark. For the other 42 years it is constantly lit up.

Uranus has only been visited by one spacecraft: NASA's Voyager 2 in 1986

VOYAGER 2

Uranus was the first planet ever to be discovered. Mercury, Venus, Mars, Jupiter and Saturn can all easily be seen with your eyes, but for Uranus it helps to have a telescope.

British astronomer William Herschel found Uranus using his telescope at home on 13 March, 1781.

Blue planet?

Uranus has a distinctive light blue appearance, but it is not made of water. Instead, methane gas in its atmosphere absorbs a lot of the red light hitting the planet. With the red light removed, the light it reflects out towards us is mostly blue.

Uranus has 27 known moons, all named after famous characters from stories by William Shakespeare or Alexander Pope, including Romeo, Juliet and Puck. Miranda is one of the oddest moons because it looks like it has been broken apart and put back together again.

TITANIA
1,578KM DIAMETER

OBERON
1,522KM DIAMETER

UMBRIEL
1,170KM DIAMETER

ARIEL
1,160KM DIAMETER

MIRANDA
470KM DIAMETER

PUCK
150KM DIAMETER

19 AU

There are 14 known Neptunian moons, with the last discovered as recently as 2013. The largest – Triton – orbits Neptune in the opposite direction to the spin of the planet. This is probably because it was an object Neptune dragged in from the Kuiper Belt.

TRITON
2,706KM DIAMETER

The Kuiper Belt is a band of small objects orbiting the Sun beyond Neptune

PROTEUS
420KM DIAMETER

NEREID
340KM DIAMETER

GALATEA
180KM DIAMETER

• FAST •
Neptune is named after the Roman god of the sea
• FACT •

GALLE
LE VERRIER
LASSELL
ARAGO
ADAMS

NEPTUNE

GALILEO
SAW NEPTUNE IN
1612 & 1613
BUT DIDN'T REALISE
IT WAS A PLANET

FAR OUT!
It takes Neptune 165 years to make one lap of the Sun because it sits so far out. The Voyager 2 space probe took 12 years to make it all the way out there! Even light from the Sun takes over four hours to make the journey (it takes just over eight minutes to reach Earth).

The rings of Neptune
Neptune has five main rings, all named after people who played an important role in the discovery of the planet: Galle, Le Verrier, Lassell, Arago and Adams. There are 42 wiggles in the Adams ring, each 30km in size, caused by the gravity of the moon Galatea.

28.3⁰
AXIS

155,600KM ROUND
AT THE EQUATOR

GAS
ATMOSPHERE

WHAT'S
INSIDE

FROZEN WATER,
AMMONIA AND
METHANE

SOLID ROCK
AND ICE
CORE

30 AU

DAY LENGTH	16 hrs 6 mins
YEAR LENGTH	165 Earth years
GRAVITY	1.12 of Earth's
AVERAGE TEMPERATURE	–228°C
DISTANCE FROM SUN	30 AU
MOONS	14

DWARF PLANETS

Just what separates a planet from everything else orbiting the Sun? The list of planets has already changed many times. When the asteroid Ceres was discovered in 1801, it was called a planet, before being removed from the list decades later. Pluto, too, was said to be a planet when it was found in 1930.

Astronomers finally wrote a list of things a planet should be or do in 2006. It has to orbit the Sun and be round in shape. Most importantly, it has to have 'cleared the neighbourhood around its orbit'. In other words, it has to be the gravitational boss of its journey around the Sun.

Pluto is not the boss of its orbit because it crosses orbits with something bigger – Neptune (see the diagram on the right). It is also greatly affected by Neptune's gravity. So astronomers invented a new term for objects like Pluto: dwarf planet. Four other objects (including Ceres) are also now officially classified as dwarf planets.

CERES

Ceres has two bright white spots that continue to puzzle astronomers.

PLUTO

NEPTUNE

SUN

Charon, largest moon of the dwarf planet Pluto

CHARON

Charon has places called Gallifrey Macula and Tardis Chasma named after The Doctor's home planet and time-machine in the TV series *Dr Who*.

PLUTO

FROZEN METHANE NITROGEN CRUST

WHAT'S INSIDE PLUTO

SOLID ROCK CORE

STYX

NIX

WATER AND ICE MANTLE

KERBEROS

DIAMETER	2,379km
DAY LENGTH	6.4 Earth days
YEAR LENGTH	248 Earth years
AVERAGE TEMPERATURE	-233°C
MOONS	5

HYDRA

119.5°
AXIS

MAKEMAKE

Makemake was found at Easter and so was known as 'Easter bunny'.

DIAMETER 1,450km
DAY LENGTH .... 22 hrs 30 mins
YEAR LENGTH ...... 306 Earth years
AVG. TEMPERATURE .... −240°C
MOONS 1

S/2015 (136472) 1

ERIS

Eris sits beyond the Kuiper Belt in a region called The Scattered Disc.

DYSNOMIA

DIAMETER 2,326km
DAY LENGTH .... 25 hrs 54 mins
YEAR LENGTH ...... 557 Earth years
AVERAGE TEMPERATURE..... −240°C
MOONS 1

NAMAKA

HAUMEA

Haumea was found at Christmas, so was nicknamed 'Santa'.

HI'IAKA

DIAMETER 1,623km
DAY LENGTH .... 3 hrs 54 mins
YEAR LENGTH ...... 285 Earth years
AVERAGE TEMPERATURE...... −241°C
MOONS 2

NASA's New Horizons probe was launched in 2006 and finally arrived at Pluto in 2015, where it took the first up-close images of this cold little world. It is continuing to journey further into the Kuiper Belt to explore more of the outer solar system.

There are almost certainly more than five dwarf planets. Other objects orbiting the Sun, like Sedna and Orcus, will probably be added to the list one day. However, we have to wait until we have good enough telescopes to prove that they are round in shape.

MILKY WAY MAGIC

On a bright, cloudless night, look up. What do you see? A band of billions of stars shimmering across the inky sky. This is our galaxy: welcome to the magical Milky Way!

IN A GALAXY NOT SO FAR, FAR AWAY...

A galaxy is the name given to a vast cluster of several hundred billion stars, interstellar gas and dust. Our solar system's eight planets (Mercury, Venus, Earth, Mars, Jupiter, Saturn, Uranus and Neptune), five dwarf planets (Pluto, Ceres, Haumea, Makemake and Eris), the Sun, the Moon, asteroids and over 200 billion stars are in the vast spiral galaxy known as the Milky Way. And the Milky Way galaxy – and billions of other galaxies – are all within the universe. Yep – your address just got waaaay longer!

Venus stardust
Cosmic house
Asteroid avenue
London
England
United Kingdom
Earth
The solar system
The milky way
The universe

Today, it is estimated that there are **2 TRILLION GALAXIES** in the observable universe.

2,000,000,000,000 GALAXIES!

Now try to imagine how many stars must exist?

MASTER OF THE GALAXY

Until the 1920s, scientists believed that all the stars in the sky were within the Milky Way. Astronomer Edwin Powell Hubble measured the distance to a distant pulsating star, and discovered it was too far away to be inside our galaxy. This helped astronomers to realise that other galaxies beyond the Milky Way galaxy existed in the Universe.

DID YOU KNOW?

Whatever your friends might say, the Milky Way isn't named after a yummy chocolate bar! Ancient Romans called the band of stars that stretches across the sky 'Via Lactea', which when translated from Latin means 'milky road' or 'milky way', and the Greeks labelled it 'Galaxias Kyklos', meaning 'milky circle'.

SPINNING AROUND

If you looked down on the Milky Way galaxy from above, it would appear as a giant spiral with four large 'arms' coming out of it. All the stars in the Milky Way, including the Sun, are constantly moving. They orbit (circle) around the galaxy's nucleus, or centre, where scientists believe there's a supermassive black hole, known as Sagittarius A* – yikes! It takes the Sun a whopping 200 million years to complete just one orbit of the nucleus, which is estimated to be 27,000 light years away, and to cross the entire Milky Way would take an amazing 100,000 light years – it's huuuuge! Most of the stars in the galaxy are single or double stars, but some 'clusters' are made up of tens of thousands of stars bunched together. Can you see star clusters when you look up at the Milky Way?

Supermassive black hole at the centre of the Milky Way galaxy

100,000 LIGHT YEARS TO CROSS IT!

THE GREAT (DARK) RIFT

▲ Milky Way galaxy as seen from New Zealand. The Great (Dark) Rift is a dark lane of dust that appears to divide the bright band of our galaxy lengthways.

★ STAR ★ MAKER

There's a lot we still don't know about the Milky Way galaxy, as a thick layer of dust obscures some of it from astronomers' view, even when they are using powerful telescopes. The Great Rift, or Dark Rift, is a long strip of cloud stretching across the Milky Way, which blocks out the light from the stars behind it. Stars are formed from clouds of gas and dust, so this Great Rift is actually a big star-making factory in the sky!

HOW IS A STAR BORN?

Like people, stars are born, grow and die

The Carina Nebula captured by the NASA Hubble Space Telescope

2 Due to gravity, the denser parts of the nebula start to attract gas and dust, and form clumps or fragments of matter inside the cloud.

A protoplanetary disc is the material surrounding a young star. Planets can form inside the discs and give rise to new planetary systems similar to our solar system.

1 Stars are formed from cold clouds of gas and dust in interstellar space called NEBULAE.

FAST⚡FACT

Gas in a nebula is mostly hydrogen formed during the Big Bang. The dust is usually created by the remains of exploding stars after they die. As you can see, the universe recycles stuff too!

3 Some of these clumps get bigger and bigger, attracting more and more matter. The cloud shrinks and becomes hotter.

A YOUNG STAR

BETELGEUSE

BELLATRIX

ALNILAM ● MINTAKA

ALNITAK ●

ORION'S BELT

ORION NEBULA

RIGEL

SAIPH ●

ORION NEBULA

On clear nights, below Orion's Belt in the Orion constellation, a whitish patch is visible to the naked eye – this is **M42** or the **ORION NEBULA**. It is a vast cloud of dust and gas where new stars form, and is like a nursery for stars.

If you look through a telescope, you'll see different young stars that have just been born. Astronomers have also found lots of protoplanetary discs.

4 In the biggest fragments of matter, gravity keeps compressing the mass of gas and dust.

It reaches a point where everything is so squished and so hot that the hydrogen atoms start colliding violently and fusing together, creating helium and giving off huge amounts of energy.

That is how a newborn star **IGNITES**

HOW DOES A STAR

MOST OF A STAR'S LIFE IS A BATTLE BETWEEN...

...the pressure of gravity on its mass that tries to crush it,

and the outward pressure of the energy from nuclear fusion that counteracts gravity.

GRAVITY **FUSION**

But when the star has no more fuel to fuse...

...gravity wins the battle and the star dies.

But how does a star die?

It depends on its mass.

LOW or MEDIUM MASS STARS

UP TO 8 TIMES
THE MASS OF THE SUN

These are the most common stars, more or less 97% of all stars that exist. They live the longest, and usually take billions of years to die. The SUN belongs to this group.

1 As they start running out of fuel, these stars get hotter and hotter inside but they also expand and get bigger.

HIGH MASS STARS

8 TO 30 TIMES
THE MASS OF THE SUN

These types of stars have more mass, therefore more pressure and heat, so they do not live as long as the ones above.

1 When they have very little fuel left, they also expand and cool, but because they are very bright to start with, they go through phases:

BLUE SUPERGIANT

YELLOW SUPERGIANT

RED SUPERGIANT

Stars in this group have the biggest mass of all, and they go through the same phases as the high mass stars, only much faster.

VERY HIGH MASS STARS

MORE THAN 30 TIMES
THE MASS OF THE SUN

DIE?

3 Once they use up all their fuel, they expel their outer layers, forming a planetary nebula, leaving only a hot and inert nucleus, a **WHITE DWARF**.

The cloud of gas and dust starts diluting and can end up becoming part of another new star.

In this state, the nucleus of the star can form heavier elements such as carbon and oxygen.

2 As their surface area increases, they cool and become red rather than yellow in colour. They turn into **RED GIANTS**.

4 This white dwarf gradually cools and in around 100 million billion years it will be cold, with no brightness, and turn into a **BLACK DWARF**, rather like a rocky planet the size of Earth. There aren't any black dwarfs yet, the universe is too young!

Red supergiants are the biggest stars in the Universe.

3 Heavy elements such as copper, gold and silver are created in a supernova.

4 The supernova leaves behind an extremely dense nucleus, a **NEUTRON STAR**, one of the densest objects in the universe.

For a few days, a supernova outshines all the stars in the galaxy

HIGH MASS

To give you an idea of the density, a neutron star with a 10km radius has the same mass as the Sun, the radius of which is 695,700km.

VERY HIGH MASS

The gravity is so huge that nothing can avoid being attracted to it, not even light.

2 When these types of stars are left with no fuel, the nucleus collapses due to the enormous gravitational pressure of their mass, and the star explodes. This then produces one of the most violent events in the universe, a **SUPERNOVA**

5 After the explosion, a large quantity of mass remains in a very small area, generating a huge gravitational field, and produces a **BLACK HOLE** instead of a neutron star.

TYPES OF STARS

HOTTER

There are many different types of stars out there, from neutron stars that are smaller than Earth to supergiants, several times bigger than our Sun

HERTZSPRUNG-RUSSELL DIAGRAM

White dwarfs, brown dwarfs, yellow dwarfs, sub-giants, red giants, blue giants, blue supergiants, neutron stars... there are lots of stars in our universe, and different ways of classifying them. Here we're using the Hertzsprung-Russell diagram that classifies stars by:

Luminosity (*brightness*)

Luminosity is measured by comparing it to the luminosity of the Sun. If a star shines twice as much as the Sun, we say that it has a luminosity of **2 L⊙**.

Temperature (*colour*)

The colour of a star is related to its surface temperature. Zero degrees Kelvin equals 273 degrees Celsius.

Size

It is not easy to represent different types of stars on a graph because of the huge differences in size. A red giant such as Betelgeuse, one of the stars in the Orion constellation, has a radius 887 times bigger than the Sun (but is only 19 times its mass).

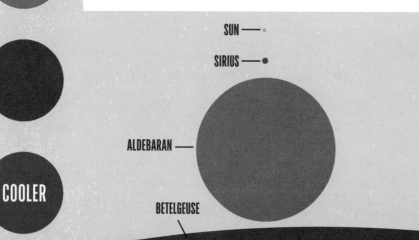

SUN —

SIRIUS —

ALDEBARAN —

BETELGEUSE

Betelgeuse has a surface temperature of **3,500 K** and a luminosity of **140,000 L⊙**.

FAST FACT

One of the biggest stars currently known about is VY Canis Majoris, which is around 2,000 times bigger than our Sun!

COOLER

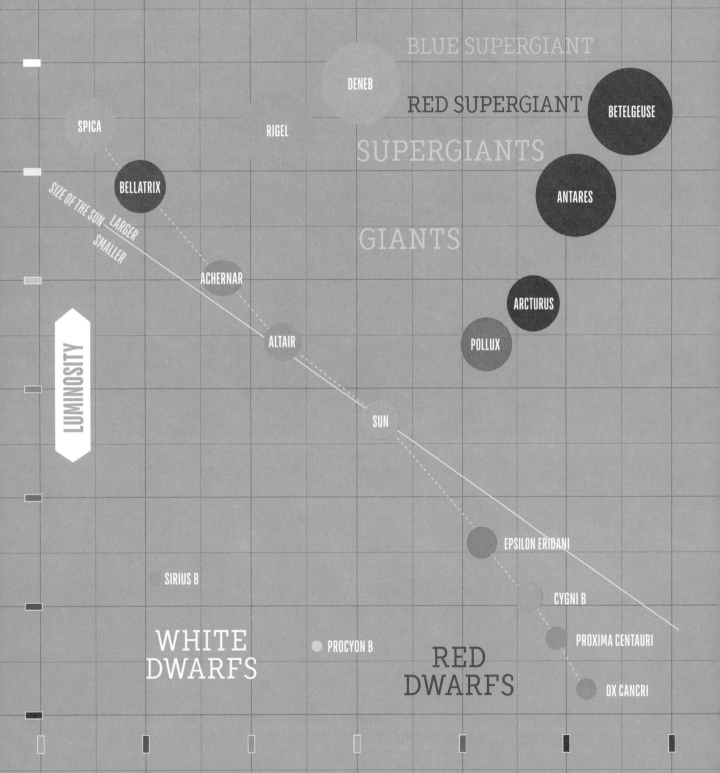

BLACK HOLES

Black holes are singular objects in the universe. Huge amounts of mass are concentrated in a black hole and it generates such an intense gravitational force that it even has the power to trap light

It's a hole in space-time that anything can fall into and nothing can escape. Its huge gravitational field is capable of attracting and swallowing anything around it; this dark giant can gobble up cosmic dust, comets, planets, stars and even light itself!

What's inside a black hole?

We have no way of knowing.

Black holes are black because, as even light cannot escape from them, they are dark and cannot be seen.

The boundary of a black hole is known as the **EVENT HORIZON**. Anything that crosses this boundary cannot come out again. We have no way of knowing what is beyond the event horizon. It is as if a kind of 'cosmic censorship' is hiding what's on the other side.

File name:
File No.

TOP SECRET

There is information inside a black hole, but we CANNOT access it.

There is thought to be a **SUPERMASSIVE** black hole at the centre of most large galaxies.

HOW A BLACK HOLE IS BORN

1 Black holes are born after a supermassive star dies in a supernova explosion.

2 If the star has sufficient mass, its gravity makes it implode and all its mass is concentrated in one point.

3 This violent event bends the surrounding space-time into a point, which generates a huge gravitational field: the one around a black hole.

EVENT HORIZON

WHAT SIZE ARE BLACK HOLES?

STELLAR-MASS BLACK HOLE

They are around 3-5 times the mass of the Sun and very small in size, with a radius of only 30km.

SUPERMASSIVE BLACK HOLE

They are millions of times the mass of the Sun, and enormous in size with a radius equivalent to planetary orbits.

BLACK HOLES 'EVAPORATE'

One of the strangest things about black holes was predicted by the great physicist Stephen Hawking. He suggested that in time black holes evaporate and start losing mass in the form of radiation until they disappear in a huge explosion. This is what is known as **HAWKING RADIATION**.

Although for this to happen, an astonishing number of years have to go by: 1,000,000,000,000,000,000... and so on, until you get to 67 zeros. (Age of the universe: 13,800,000,000 years!)

STEPHEN HAWKING

HOW TO DETECT THEM

We cannot directly see black holes but we can observe the effects that they produce due to the huge gravity that they generate. For example, they can act as gravitational lenses, bending the light of a star behind them to make it visible. We can also see stars orbiting around something invisible. That is how we know that there is a black hole attracting them with its huge gravity, although we cannot see it.

WHAT HAPPENS IF YOU FALL INTO A BLACK HOLE?

Imagine that one day you trip and fall into a black hole. First of all, it's pretty unlucky. But what happens to you when you cross the event horizon?

It's no use calling to someone outside for help. They'll never be able to see or hear you, because no signals, not even from light, can escape a black hole!

So you fall in and as you approach the centre, the pull of gravity is more intense on your feet than your head. It would be like two giants pulling you, and you would start stretching like a piece of spaghetti. You would end up being ripped into shreds!

Mapping the sky

Meteor showers can be seen all over the night sky but usually seem to burst towards us from the same point each year, which can help when you try to look for them. Some showers are named after the star or constellation of stars that they appear to come from.

DID YOU KNOW?

When a **METEOROID** travels all the way through the Earth's atmosphere and lands on the ground, it's called a **METEORITE**.

Shooting STARS

Outer space may feel a long way away, but meteor showers can be seen easily from Earth

What is a meteoroid?

A shooting star isn't really a star at all – it's a meteoroid, or space rock, from the tail of a comet or asteroid. Comets orbit the Sun just like planets do. When they get close to it, the heat burns off some of the ice from their surface, leaving a trail of dust and rocks. When these rocks enter the Earth's atmosphere, they get very hot and release a burning trail. They are then called meteors. This is what we're really seeing when we spot a shooting star!

Cosmic calendar

While the dates for meteor showers is the same each year, the phase the Moon is in during them changes. To be able to see meteor showers clearly, the night sky needs to be dark. This means the best chance to enjoy a sky full of shooting stars is on or either side of a new Moon.

You can check a lunar calendar online to find out when these fall.

MOON CALENDAR

Sunday	Monday	Tuesday	Wednesday	Thursday	Friday	Saturday
				01	02	03
04	05	06	07	08	09	10
11	12	13	14	15	16	17
18	19	20	21	22	23	24
25	26	27	28	29	30	

Meteor showers

When a lot of meteoroids enter the Earth's atmosphere at once, we call it a meteor shower. This usually happens when the Earth passes through the trail of dust left by a comet or asteroid. Because comets and asteroids move around the Sun on a fixed path, just like the Earth does, we pass through each one's trail at the same time each year on our journey around the Sun.

DATES AND DEETS
Here's the lowdown on the major meteor showers

WINTER

GEMINIDS

WHAT? Considered the best meteor shower to view with up to 120 brightly coloured meteors per hour from the trail of an asteroid called Phaeton

WHERE? From the constellation Gemini

QUADRANTIDS

WHAT? A shower of up to 40 blue meteors per hour from the trail of an extinct comet

WHERE? Between the constellation Boötes, also known as the Herdsman, and the Plough, or Big Dipper

SPRING

LYRIDS

WHAT? A shower of up to 20 meteors per hour with bright dust trails from comet Thatcher

WHERE? From the constellation Lyra

SUMMER

PERSEIDS

WHAT? An exciting shower with up to 60 fast meteors per hour from comet Swift-Tuttle

WHERE? From the constellation Perseus

AUTUMN

ORIONIDS

WHAT? A shower of up to 20 fine-trained meteors per hour from Halley's Comet

WHERE? From the constellation Orion

LEONIDS

WHAT? A shower from the comet Tempel-Tuttle of up to 15 bright meteors per hour but peaking every 33 years when hundreds per hour can be seen. The next peak is around 2034

WHERE? From the constellation Leo

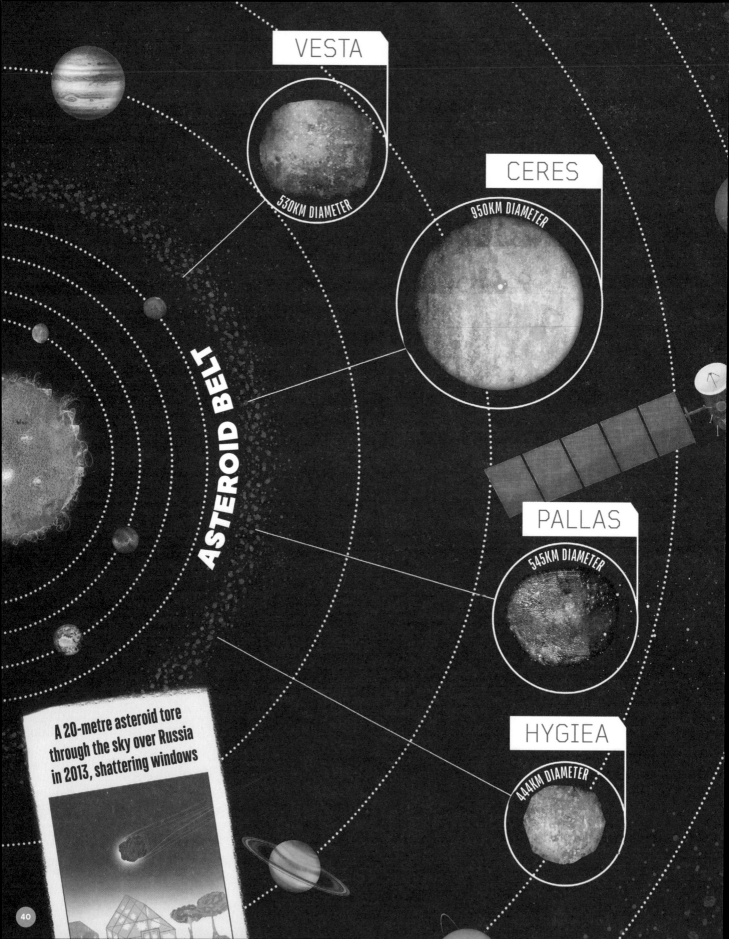

VESTA

530KM DIAMETER

CERES

950KM DIAMETER

PALLAS

545KM DIAMETER

HYGIEA

444KM DIAMETER

ASTEROID BELT

A 20-metre asteroid tore through the sky over Russia in 2013, shattering windows

KUIPER BELT

Astronomers keep a close eye on asteroids because they can be dangerous. Sixty-six million years ago an asteroid the size of a city hit the coast of Mexico, wiping out the dinosaurs and killing off more than 70% of all life on Earth! Today we'd see it coming.

WHAT ARE ASTEROIDS?

Asteroids are leftover building blocks from the formation of the rocky planets. Most of the rocks there have been kicked out over time, and today the whole Asteroid Belt weighs just 4% of the Moon (or less than 25% of Pluto). They range from 950km across to the size of dust and pebbles

CHAPTER 2

THE SPACE RACE

Would you journey to the Moon? What about Mars? Space travel has been going on for over half a century and there are exciting new manned missions planned to other planets in the not-too-distant future. Read on to find out more about the Space Race and Apollo 11 Moon landing, what it's like to live on the International Space Station and the present and future of manned space exploration...

RACE TO SPACE

1897

Russian scientist **KONSTANTIN TSIOLKOVSKY** worked out the science of rockets in 1897.

1942

The **V-2 ROCKET** was the first to cross the Kármán line – the boundary that marks the beginning of outer space – in 1942.

V-2 ROCKET

YURI GAGARIN

1962

The **MARINER 2** space probe was the first successful interplanetary spacecraft in 1962.

1961

The Soviets were the first to put a person in space. On 12 April, 1961, cosmonaut **YURI GAGARIN** orbited the Earth once before landing in the middle of a field close to a farmer and his daughter. Yuri became an instant, worldwide celebrity.

CCCP

VALENTINA TERESHKOVA

MARINER 2

1963

The first woman in space was Soviet cosmonaut **VALENTINA TERESHKOVA** in 1963.

INTERNATIONAL SPACE STATION

1998

In recent years, space exploration has been more of a joint effort between many countries working together. The **INTERNATIONAL SPACE STATION** is home to a multinational crew of astronauts sharing knowledge about how best to work in space. They are learning how to survive in space for long periods of time.

VOYAGER 1

ROSETTA PROBE

PHILAE LANDER

2012

In 2012, the **VOYAGER 1** probe entered interstellar space.

2014

In 2014, the European Space Agency's **ROSETTA** probe made an historic landing on a comet, dropping the **PHILAE** lander onto the nucleus.

1947

The first animals in space were fruit flies, launched by the US in 1947.

SPACE FLIES

1949

ALBERT II

ALBERT II became the first monkey in space in 1949.

1957

SPUTNIK 1

In 1957, the Soviet Union sent **SPUTNIK 1** into space – the first human-made object to orbit the Earth. It stayed in orbit for three months before burning up in the atmosphere. It sent out a series of radio beeps so that it could be tracked from the ground.

LUNA 2

1959

In 1959, **LUNA 2** became the first spacecraft to reach the surface of the Moon.

NEIL ARMSTRONG

1965

Cosmonaut **ALEXEI LEONOV** performed the first space walk in 1965.

DISCOVERY

1969

The Americans finally achieved an important first in space exploration when they successfully landed people on the Moon in July 1969. **NEIL ARMSTRONG** stepped off the ladder of the landing module and uttered the famous words *'It's one small step for [a] man, one giant leap for mankind.'*

1984

ALEXEI LEONOV

DISCOVERY (OV-103) was NASA's third space shuttle orbiter and made its first mission in 1984. It would go on to complete over 30 missions, more than any other orbiter.

BLUE ORIGIN

2015

In 2015, lettuce became the first food to be grown in space.

2018

In 2018, **SPACEX** founder Elon Musk launched his red sports car into space on the **FALCON HEAVY** rocket.

2021

Amazon founder Jeff Bezos makes his first trip to space on Blue Origin's New Shepard vehicle

MICHAEL COLLINS

Role: Command Module Pilot

Often forgotten, Michael flew the Apollo's command module around the Moon while Buzz and Neil went walkabout. Born in Rome, he became a test pilot in the US Air Force and in 1963 was chosen to train as an astronaut.

NEIL ARMSTRONG

Role: Commander

Neil loved aeroplanes and space as a kid, so much so that he got his student pilot's licence when he was just 16 – before he could even drive! He was 38 when he flew to the Moon.

FIRST MEN ON THE MOON

These brave astronauts were the first to land on the Moon! Read about how three young Americans made it into space... and came back lunar legends

SATURN V ROCKET

THE COMMAND MODULE
(codenamed Columbia) was the main ship, where the astronauts spent most of the journey

THE SERVICE MODULE
provided power and storage for the Command Module

THE LUNAR MODULE
(codenamed Eagle) used by Neil and Buzz to get to the Moon's surface

THIRD STAGE
These final engines were jettisoned after the aircraft escaped Earth's gravity, around 300km above the Earth's surface

SECOND STAGE
These engines took the rocket above them to around 190km above the Earth's surface before being jettisoned

FIRST STAGE
These big, powerful engines propelled the whole rocket to around 65km above the Earth's surface and then were jettisoned when their fuel was used up

SATURN V:
111 METRES TALL
2.8 MILLION KG
EQUAL TO
x400

BUZZ ALDRIN

Role: Lunar Module Pilot

Buzz Aldrin served in the US Air Force. In 1966, he completed a two-and-a-half-hour spacewalk during the Gemini 12 space mission and while there he took the first ever 'selfie' in space! Can you believe his mum's maiden name was Moon?

APOLLO 11

UP AND AWAY!

16 JULY 1969 *blast off!*

Apollo 11 blasted off from Cape Kennedy at 9.32am with its three astronauts onboard. Filled with nearly a million gallons of fuel, the moment of ignition must have been pretty nail-biting!

3 hours later

The rocket swung once around Earth and zoomed off towards the Moon. The astronauts had to perform some tricky manoeuvres, all the while hurtling along at **32,000KM/H**

▲
Members of the Kennedy Space Center team inside the Launch Control Center watch the Apollo 11 liftoff through a window

19 JULY

It took three days to travel the 384,400km between the Earth and the Moon. On the third day, the astronauts had the very difficult job of getting Apollo 11 into the Moon's orbit, around 100km above the lunar surface.

20 JULY

The next day, Neil and Buzz climbed into the Eagle, leaving Michael to wait nervously in orbit. In the most dangerous part of the mission, the Eagle separated from Columbia and Neil and Buzz piloted it for two hours to the Moon's surface. The Eagle was so small, there was no room for seats, so they stood up the whole way!

2 hours later

At the last minute, almost out of fuel, Neil realised that the automatic landing program was going to land them in a rocky crater, filled with huge boulders! Neil quickly took over the controls and sped up, so the Eagle would miss the crater and land just beyond it.

THE LANDING

Neil had to stay calm as an alarm began to sound and Mission Control said there was just 30 seconds of fuel left! 'The Eagle has landed,' said Neil when they finally touched down at 4.17pm. Phew!

6 hours later

As the commander, Neil was lucky enough to go first. He stepped off the ladder onto the Moon and famously said: 'That's one small step for man, one giant leap for mankind!' (although later Neil insisted he actually said 'one small step for a man'!). Twenty minutes later Buzz followed.

ON THE MOON

Neil and Buzz spent nearly a whole day on the Moon. They took photos and collected soil and moon rocks. Neil was the first person to step on the Moon, but Buzz was the first man to go to the toilet on it!

3 DAYS TO TRAVEL **384,400 KM**

Crater photographed by Apollo 11 crew near landing site

Astronaut Buzz Aldrin descends from the Lunar Module ▼

> ## That's one small step for man, one giant leap for mankind
> **NEIL ARMSTRONG**

91 DAYS
How long it would take to walk around the whole of the Moon in one go. **Nobody's tried it!**

Forever feet
There's no weather on the Moon, which means Neil and Buzz's footprints are still there today!

DID YOU KNOW?

The area Neil chose to land on the Moon is called the Sea of Tranquility – but it's not really a sea. Years ago, ancient astronomers looked at the Moon and thought patches of volcanic rock were seas and oceans – they were wrong!

21 JULY

Mission Control watched anxiously as Neil and Buzz prepared for lift off. If the engine didn't ignite, they'd be stuck! America's President Nixon had even prepared a speech in case they didn't make it back alive. Thankfully everything worked perfectly and after docking with Columbia, the crew set course for home.

24 JULY

Three days later, the Command Module re-entered the Earth's atmosphere, travelling at 38,600km/h! They had to come in at exactly the right angle or the capsule would be burnt to a crisp. After three minutes of no communication, the whole world breathed a sigh of relief when Neil announced a safe re-entry.

SPLASHDOWN

Eight days after launch, Apollo 11 splashed down in the Pacific Ocean. Neil, Buzz and Michael had to quarantine for 21 days to make sure they hadn't brought back any dangerous Moon bacteria!

650 MILLION PEOPLE ACROSS THE WORLD WATCHED THE MOON LANDING ON TV

NEW YORK CITY welcomes Apollo 11 crewmen in a showering of ticker tape down Broadway and Park Avenue in a parade termed as the largest in the city's history

FIRST MEN ON THE MOON
APOLLO 11
COLLINS ARMSTRONG ALDRIN
JULY 20TH
CAPE KENNEDY, FLORIDA 1969

Crew members typically spend six months on board, although some have stayed as long as a year! They help us understand the effects that long stays in outer space have on the human body.

The solar panels on the ISS are so reflective that you can easily see it from the ground at night. Brighter than any of the planets, it isn't above you for very long, though. Travelling at speeds of 28,000km/h, it orbits the whole planet in just 92 minutes, and soon disappears from view.

WEIGHS 420,000KG
THAT'S MORE THAN
3 ADULT WHALES

CANADARM2

DESTINY LABORATORY

EUROPEAN MODULE

HARMONY MODULE

ALL ABOARD THE

International Space Station

CREW MEMBERS SEE

16 SUNSETS & SUNRISES

EVERY SINGLE DAY

The International Space Station (ISS) is a home for humanity in orbit. It has been permanently inhabited by astronauts since November 2000

ZARYA SERVICE MODULE

ZVEZDA SERVICE MODULE

UNITY MODULE

LABORATORY MODULE

KIBŌ OUTER RESEARCH PLATFORM

KIBŌ RESEARCH MODULE

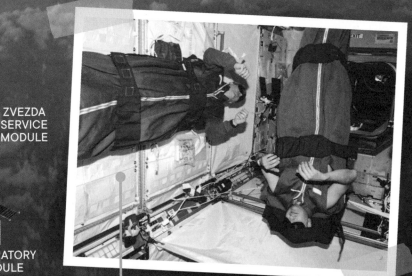

Astronauts on the ISS sleep inside sleeping bags tied to the station's walls.

MOST EXPENSIVE MAN-MADE OBJECT

150 BILLION DOLLARS

Astronauts aboard the ISS float around because they are weightless. However, this does not mean there is no gravity in space. If that were true, then there'd be nothing stopping the Space Station from floating off into the solar system. Astronauts float because they are in free fall around the planet.

▲ Flight Engineers Thomas Pesquet and Megan McArthur are pictured inside the cupola, the International Space Station's 'window to the world'.

4 2ND STAGE SEPARATION
(5 MINUTES)

- 200KM
- 170KM

Only **24** astronauts have left Low-Earth Orbit (LEO)

CAPSULE OPENS FOR JOURNEY AND DOCKING

5 3RD STAGE SEPARATION
(9 MINUTES)

3 FAIRING JETTISONED
(3 MINUTES)

- KÁRMÁN LINE
- 100KM

TO SPACE AND BACK

How do astronauts and cosmonauts get to and from the International Space Station? In Soyuz rockets!

2 BOOSTERS SEPARATION
(2 MINUTES)

- 40KM

Fewer than **600** PEOPLE have ever launched into space!

Re-entering Earth's atmosphere at the end of a mission is just as dangerous as launching into space in the first place. Friction with the air heats the outside of the capsule to 2,000°C. The angle of approach is crucial – too steep and you'll burn up completely!

1 TAKE-OFF
(12 SECONDS)

EXOSPHERE
690–190,000KM

THERMOSPHERE 85–690KM

6 TIME IN ORBIT

7 RETURN TO EARTH

KÁRMÁN
LINE

100KM

**PARTS BURN UP
IN ATMOSPHERE**

MESOSPHERE 50–85KM

**3 HOURS TO
RETURN
TO EARTH**

STRATOSPHERE 20–50KM

**8
TOUCHDOWN**

TROPOSPHERE 0–20KM

As the Soyuz capsule approaches the ground, parachutes are deployed to slow you down. However, you still hit the ground with a mighty bump. Helicopters land nearby with a rescue team to help you out of the capsule as you get used to gravity again after months of weightlessness in space.

The Soyuz TMA-20M spacecraft is seen as it lands with Expedition 48 crew members near the town of Zhezkazgan, Kazakhstan, 7 September, 2016.

SUITED & BOOTED

Ready for a walk on the wild side? Spacesuits keep astronauts safe in extreme conditions! If you're planning a spacewalk, you're going to need an EVA suit

LIFE SUPPORT SYSTEM

The backpack may look bulky but it's filled with everything astronauts need to explore! A huge rechargeable battery powers the suit's tech while a fan and a water tank keep astronauts cool.

$500 MILLION

How much a spacesuit can cost... *think about all the technology scientists have to pack in!*

HELMET

A window to other worlds, the helmet is made of strong plastic so it's robust but won't shatter. Inside, you'll find a small foam block for nose scratching and a sun-blocking visor... just like sunglasses!

GLOVES

An astronaut's gloves must serve two purposes: protect them and let them work effectively. That's why for years designers built plaster casts of each crew members' hands!

UPPER TORSO

The sleeveless chest piece of an EVA spacesuit has to be lightweight but also incredibly strong! Connecting the astronaut's soft under layers to life support systems, it's the first line of defence.

LOWER TORSO

While the hard upper casing keeps the wearer safe, this section lets them move about freely on missions. In the past, astronauts have had to hop in low gravity to get around. New suits will thankfully be fully flexible!

COOLING GARMENT

One section of the spacesuit you can't see is a sandwiched system that works to keep astronauts comfortable. The cooling garment works like your radiator at home to circulate water around the body.

OUT IN THE STARS

Astronauts call the spacewalk an EVA – an 'extra-vehicular activity'. There's so much tech inside an EVA spacesuit that it's almost a human-shaped spaceship itself.

Safe space

There's a lot to deal with in deep space! Debris, dust, extreme temperatures and even radiation threaten astronauts on every trip. First and foremost, EVA suits need to copy the Earth's atmosphere effectively!

Super senses

Bright lights help the suit's wearer see in space, but sensors are always looking inside too to keep them healthy! Spacesuits measure carbon dioxide, radiation levels and temperature and make sure there's always enough oxygen.

Getting ready

There are 25 steps to putting on an EVA spacesuit! They're modular, meaning they come in multiple parts – the process of piecing it all together allows space travellers to perform vital safety checks.

Built to last

The exterior layers of modern suits are made of Nomex, Kevlar and Teflon – the toughest man-made materials around. This means it's super rare for them to tear.

MISSION DANGER

They say that in space no one can hear you scream! That's because there's no air in space. It's called a 'vacuum', and sound waves can't travel through it. This also makes exploring space pretty risky! That's why scientists spend years creating ships, suits and special tools so humans can survive while they're there. Here are just a few of the dangers that astronauts face...

DANGER #1:
TEMPERATURE

What's the problem? Temperatures in space can vary from super cold (-150°C) to incredibly hot (+120°C), depending on whether you're in sunlight or not. Also, when ships re-enter the Earth's atmosphere, friction can mean temperatures shoot up to 1,650°C!

What can we do about it? Spacesuits and crafts are designed to keep temperatures at a comfortable 20°C. Ships are also lined with heat-proof tiles and built to reflect heat and absorb energy.

· RISK ·
7
· RATING ·

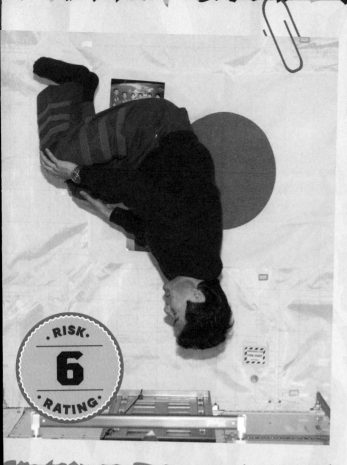

DANGER #2:
GRAVITY

What's the problem? There are lots! To begin with, gravity makes taking off tricky – if an object on the Earth's surface wants to fly free, it needs to travel faster than 40,000km/h. Plus the further astronauts get from Earth, the less gravitational force there is. Out in space, objects don't fall, they float. If they jump up, they don't come back down. This can make astronauts feel sick. And spacecrafts have to be driven differently, too. If an astronaut fires a thruster on a ship, the ship shoots forward. But when the thruster stops, the ship keeps going at the same speed. The only way to stop it is to fire a thruster in the opposite direction.

What can we do about it? Astronauts go to space gym. They're given two hours a day to exercise, which helps them cope with the effects of gravity. They train before they go, too, by practising in special aircrafts. Scientists are also looking at ways to create artificial gravity.

RISK 6 RATING

DANGER #3:
DISTANCE

RISK 5 RATING

What's the problem? Mars is 225 million km from Earth – pretty far, huh? It would take about three days to get to the Moon, but it'd take astronauts a year and a half to get to Mars and back. Basically, our ships are way too slow. Plus when they're in deep space, there can be a communication delay of up to 20 minutes, so placing an emergency call is tricky.

What can we do about it? Scientists are looking at ways to make rockets go faster, so they could get to Mars quicker. Researchers also plan ahead for disasters and predict what could go wrong, so they have everything on board to try and solve the problem. Planning is key.

DANGER #4:
RADIATION

What's the problem? Have you heard of radiation? It's energy that moves from one place to another. Through space, radiation waves travel at a speed of almost 300,000km per second. Without the protection of Earth's atmosphere, these waves can affect people's bodies and make them sick.

What can we do about it? Cleverly designed suits and ships mean astronauts aren't directly exposed to radiation. Space stations also have extra shielding in the places people spend the most time: the sleeping quarters and the galley.

RISK 8 RATING

DANGER #5:
FOOD AND WATER

What's the problem? It's pretty hard to grow your own food with no gravity – imagine pouring water, it would just float around rather than trickle into the soil! And transporting anything to space stations is expensive, especially water, because it's so heavy.
What can we do about it? Astronauts take lots and lots of food with them, which is packaged in tight pouches that don't take up too much space (and won't spill!). Sometimes their food is powdered like baby food – all they have to do is add water via a special tube.

Astronauts also create water by collecting moisture from breath, sweat and pee! They recycle it through a system using acid, then drink it like bottled water at home. Mmmm... tasty!

.RISK.
8
.RATING.

DANGER #6:
SPACE DEBRIS

What's the problem? Congratulations! You've successfully launched your rocket into orbit. But before you break into outer space, a rogue bit of broken satellite comes out of nowhere and hits your fuel tank. This is the problem with space debris. Right now space surveillance experts are watching more than 27,000 objects – each at least the size of a tennis ball – hurtling around Earth at speeds of more than 28,000km/h! Think of it like a space junkyard.
What can we do about it? One solution is called 'de-orbiting' – which basically means pushing the junk out of orbit and into the Earth's atmosphere, where it will burn up! Space surveillance experts also do a good job of alerting pilots what debris may be nearby.

.RISK.
7
.RATING.

FACT EVEN TINY OBJECTS CAN CAUSE DAMAGE. LOTS OF SPACE SHUTTLE WINDOWS HAVE HAD TO BE REPLACED BECAUSE THEY WERE HIT BY FLECKS OF PAINT

DANGER #7:
ATMOSPHERE

RISK 10 RATING

What's the problem? There's no air in space, and we need air to breathe!
What can we do about it? Astronauts bring oxygen from Earth when they go on a space mission and sometimes they make it by running electricity through water. But this is also where spacesuits come in – astronauts get oxygen into their suits from their backpacks! They usually have two oxygen tanks in there, which allows them to breathe in outer space for about eight hours.

FACT THE INTERNATIONAL SPACE STATION GETS REGULAR SHIPMENTS OF OXYGEN FROM EARTH TO KEEP THEIR SUPPLIES TOPPED UP

'**HOUSTON, WE HAVE A PROBLEM**'

Do you recognise that phrase? The now-famous quote comes from the Apollo 13 mission. Apollo 13 was meant to be the third mission to land on the Moon – but it didn't quite go to plan.

The mission had to be cancelled, because the oxygen tank broke! Instead, the crew looped around the Moon and returned to Earth. Apparently astronauts John Swigert and James Lovell actually said: 'Houston, we've had a problem here.' Still, the mission was called 'a successful failure' because they returned home safely. Phew!

NO SPACESUIT? Uh-oh!

You'd lose consciousness in about **15 seconds**, die after **90 seconds** and freeze solid within **12-26 hours**!

DANGER #8:
LONELINESS

RISK 4 RATING

What's the problem? Going to space might sound fun, but it can also be lonely! Astronauts are only around a few other people, in a small area – sometimes for a very long time. If they're away for three years, that's more than 1,000 days away from family and friends!
What can we do about it? Scientists are looking at creating virtual reality simulations to make astronauts feel as if they're in a relaxing environment that's a bit more like home.

FAR-OUT FOOD

Feeling hungry? Learn what it's like to eat like an astronaut as we process the facts about space food. Bon appetit!

Jelly dish

Think of space food and you might imagine pills or toothpaste-like tubes full of not-so-tasty pastes. Not anymore! These days nutritionists prepare astronauts three carefully balanced meals a day. The menu on board the International Space Station includes more than 100 items, from vegetables and fruit to pre-prepared meals and desserts that come in special pouches.

Up in the air

Were you aware you can eat upside down? It means astronauts can enjoy meals in zero gravity! Digestion is designed with every angle in mind, and your stomach can do its job anywhere. But being in zero gravity means food can get away from you! Straws have tiny clamps to stop bubbles from getting out and all washing up is done with wipes. Astronauts strap themselves into chairs with thigh and foot supports and eat from magnetised trays and cutlery.

Hot stuff

There's some serious science in space food! To make sure meals like macaroni cheese don't spoil and make astronauts sick, scientists freeze-dry them in pouches and then hot water can be added in space. If a food can't be freeze-dried then it's 'thermostabilised' instead – heated to over 100°C and quickly packaged in air-tight containers! This destroys any germs and makes it last longer.

Spice travel

Space can really mess with your senses. On Earth, gravity pulls the fluid in your body into your legs. In space, fluid moves freely throughout the body, which can give astronauts a puffy face and affect their sense of smell. To give food more flavour, astronauts often add super hot sauces to it!

Oh crumbs!

Space travellers aren't allowed food that will clog up the cockpit, so bread's off the menu! No crisps are allowed either, but soup is available. Surface tension keeps it on the spoon! Salt and pepper are also banned in case they float away and get into the ventilation system or stick in someone's eyeball! So how do astronauts season their food? Using liquid salt and pepper, of course!

TOILET TIME

Stand by for blast off! Even astronauts need the loo... ever wondered how they go? Of course you have!

This sucks!

Think about it: taking a toilet break in space could get messy... fast! Space-based toilets work like vacuum cleaners – they just hoover waste right up.

Boldly go

Bathrooms in space can get pretty cramped when you can't sit down! Astronauts' waste collectors are called Zero Gravity Toilets, and they're shaped to catch floaters.

Silent but violent

Farts smell even worse in space shuttles! That's because there's no air to disperse them, so they really hang around. Everyone will know who dealt it in space. Gross!

SNACK

TO THE MOON AND BACK

Can you imagine walking on the Moon? One day, you might be able to. A long time ago (between 1968 and 1972!) there were nine missions to the Moon and 12 men walked on the surface. Now, there's a plan to get people back there...

WHY ARE THEY GOING?

NASA's programme to get people back to the Moon is called **ARTEMIS**. It aims to set up a permanent base on the surface of the Moon and in orbit around it by 2024. And because the only astronauts to have been to the Moon so far have all been white and male...

ARTEMIS

ARTEMIS HOPES TO LAND THE **FIRST** WOMAN & PERSON OF COLOUR ON THE MOON

→ SOUTH POLE

Who will go?

NASA has selected 18 astronauts to fly back to the Moon – nine men and nine women. Former US Vice President Mike Pence called them 'heroes who will carry us to the Moon and beyond'. What a job!

> We're going back to the Moon for scientific discovery, economic benefits and inspiration for a new generation of explorers: the Artemis Generation.
>
> **NASA**

LATEST BUDGET
$25 BILLION
AND COUNTING...

COULD YOU BE AN ASTRONAUT?

You'd be trained to...

✓ SPACEWALK

✓ FLY A JET

✓ OPERATE ROBOTIC ARMS

✓ SPEAK RUSSIAN

✓ COPE WITH ISOLATION

✓ WEAR A VERY HEAVY SUIT!

5.582 4.351 3.658
5.238 4.808 8.703
3.332 6.821 3.660
4.084 6.519 7.078
7.214 5.284 8.227
3.429 6.218 4.101
7.543 7.880 6.729
5.904 6.570 6.844

HOW WILL THEY GET THERE?
With these **FOUR** things...

The Crew Module
It has the largest crew cabin NASA has ever made! This is where the astronauts sit and it can hold up to six of them, giving them a safe space to stay during launch and landing. This is the only part of the spacecraft that returns after a mission.

The Launch Abort System
This is designed to keep the astronauts safe during launch and when the spacecraft first starts coming back down to Earth. It can be turned on within milliseconds to begin a safe landing. This is a key reason Orion is thought to be the safest spacecraft ever built.

1 THE ORION SPACECRAFT

* Orion is named after one of the largest constellations in the night sky
* It's seen as the 'stepping stone' to transport humans to Mars – because of how far it can travel into space
* **43,452KM/H** is the maximum speed needed to blast Orion into deep space. Compare that to 113km/h, which is the maximum speed that cars are allowed to travel on motorways on Earth!
* NASA has spent $23.7 billion developing the Orion spacecraft – that's just over £17 billion. Eek!

* It has what's called a 'heat shield' that protects astronauts from really, really high temperatures (2,204°C!) when they come back to Earth – that's even hotter than lava!
* During the descent, Orion will travel 35 times faster than a speeding bullet!
* To help the spacecraft slow down for landing, it has lots of parachutes – eight small ones and three ginormous ones. The larger parachutes combined would almost cover a football field.

The Service Module
This is where the spacecraft gets its power. It also provides essentials such as water, oxygen, nitrogen and heat to support the crew module.

2 THE SPACE LAUNCH SYSTEM (SLS)

* The huge rocket that will launch Orion to the Moon will be the 'most powerful rocket in the world'.
* It will provide the power to help Orion reach a speed of **39,429** KILOMETRES PER HOUR!

* It stands taller than the Statue of Liberty, which is 93m.
* This super heavy-lift rocket will be able to carry almost 180,000kg.
  It will cost $800 million per launch!

◄ 93 METRES TALL ►

3 THE LUNAR GATEWAY

* The gateway is a small space station that will orbit the Moon.
* It'll be where the astronauts live and work.
* It's like an office that provides support to those exploring on the Moon's surface.
* It could be in orbit for up to 10 years!

4 THE LUNAR LANDER

* This is the final stage of transport in the journey to the Moon.
* The lunar lander is a spacecraft that will carry astronauts from the gateway onto the surface of the Moon and back again.

WHEN WILL THEY GO?

ARTEMIS I This first test flight sent an unmanned Orion spacecraft and Space Launch System to the Moon and back.

ARTEMIS II (Pictured here) Planned for launch in 2024, a four-person crew will fly an Orion spacecraft past the Moon and back again.

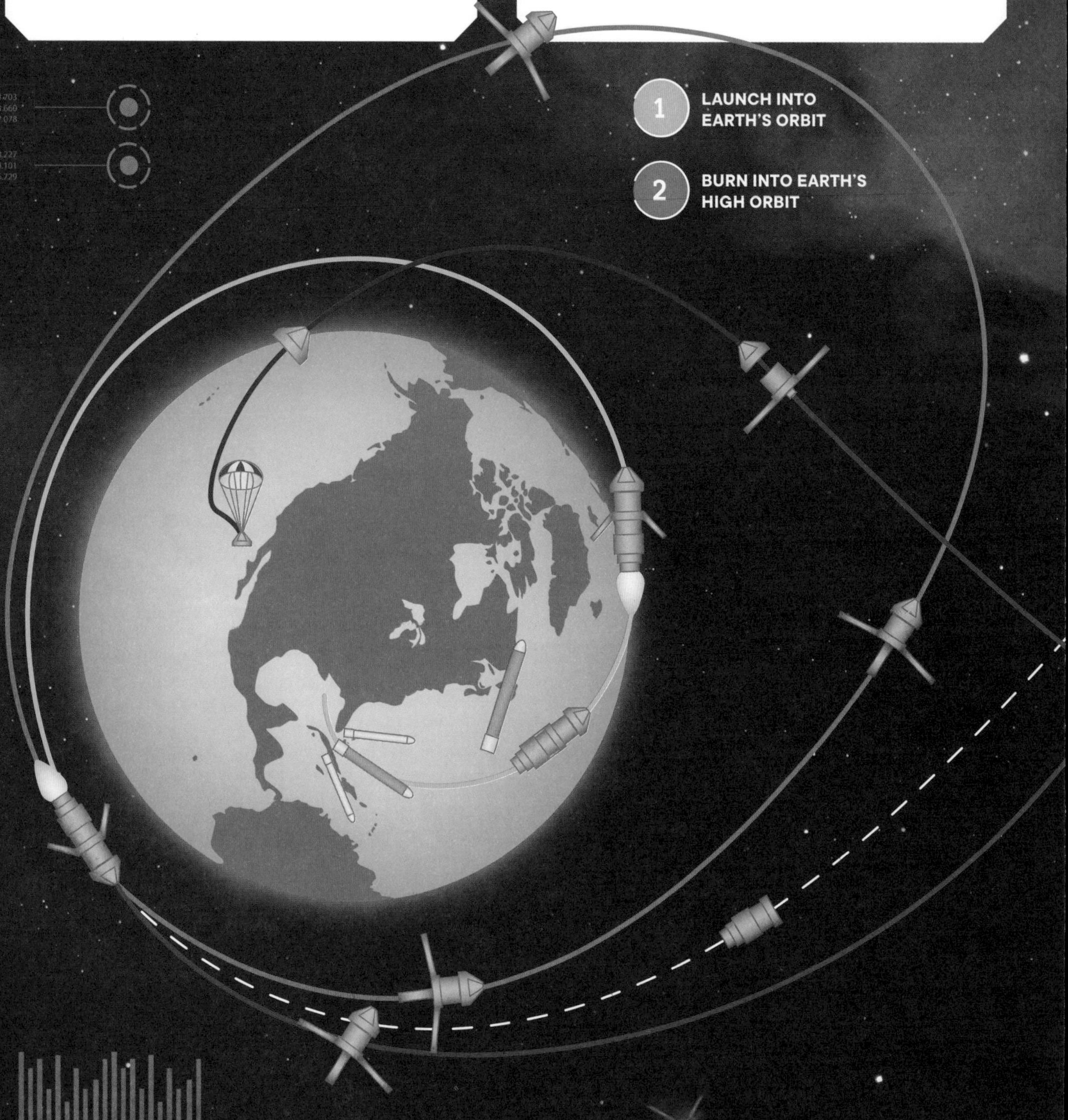

5.238 4.808 8.703
3.332 6.821 3.660
4.084 6.519 7.078

7.214 5.284 8.227
3.429 6.218 4.101
7.543 7.880 6.729

1 LAUNCH INTO EARTH'S ORBIT

2 BURN INTO EARTH'S HIGH ORBIT

Before Artemis carries people back to the Moon, NASA will test the rockets and equipment to make sure everything works and is as safe as possible.

ARTEMIS III In 2025 four astronauts on board an Orion spacecraft will dock with the Lunar Gateway and stay in space for a month. The Lunar Lander will take two of the astronauts to the Moon's South Pole, an area that humans have never set foot on! One of them will be the first woman astronaut on the Moon.

ARTEMIS

3 FOUR-DAY JOURNEY TO THE MOON

4 LUNAR FLYBY FOLLOWED BY FOUR-DAY RETURN JOURNEY

5 DESCENT TO EARTH

NEXT UP, MARS!

Once the programme has learned all it can about the Moon, the team hopes to take the next big step: sending astronauts to Mars. The Red Planet is around 225 million km away from Earth and it would take nine months to get there!

WANNA GO TO MARS?

Would you leave your home on Earth to go and live on another planet like Mars?

WOULD YOU JOIN AN EXPEDITION TO MARS?

At its closest approach to Earth in 2020, Mars was still a whopping 62.1 million kilometres away, but it's actually the most accessible planet in our solar system, so it's a good place for humans to explore and learn more about space. NASA has begun searching for suitable locations to land humans on Mars by 2033 – and also to allow them to live and work there in the future. Meanwhile, inventor Elon Musk's SpaceX programme has plans to build settlements on Mars as early as 2026.

HOTEL

MARS 345

Mars is much smaller than Earth at just **1/10** of its mass. Gravity on Mars is about **38%** of that on Earth, which means you could lift heavy things more easily, and bounce around!

Welcome to your MARS MANSION

Your home on Mars will need to be super tough to survive the planet's harsh conditions, atmospheric pressure and extreme temperatures. The AI SpaceFactory won the NASA Centennial Challenge to develop the design and technologies to build on Mars. The egg-shaped four-level home, Marsha, uses advanced 3D printing technologies, combining basalt rock and renewable bioplastic made from plants that could be grown on Mars, and is strong enough to protect its inhabitants from harmful cosmic and solar radiation.

Photo: AI SpaceFactory and Plomp

WHAT WE NEED TO LIVE ON MARS

OXYGEN

Humans need oxygen to breathe. The air in Earth's atmosphere is made up of around 78% nitrogen and 21% oxygen, plus small amounts of other gases. The atmosphere on Mars is made up of 95% carbon dioxide and less than 1% oxygen, so people cannot naturally breathe the air. The Mars 2020 rover mission is undertaking a Mars Oxygen In-Situ Resource Utilisation Experiment (MOXIE) to produce oxygen from the planet's atmosphere. Genius!

WATER

Important for all life on Earth, humans need to consume water to survive. Up to 55-60% of an adult's human body is water, and it's vital to keep our body functioning and healthy. Previous Mars missions have discovered what is believed to be large ice deposits just beneath the planet's surface, and scientists are investigating methods of turning this ice into water for human visitors. The planet may also be home to underground saltwater lakes.

FOOD

Like Earth, Mars rotates on an axis, so experiences night and day, with light from the Sun reaching the planet, but as Mars is over 80 million kilometres further from the Sun, the amount of light and heat reaching the planet is much less, so plants will need to be grown inside controlled environments, like greenhouses. And while the soil on Mars contains nutrients similar to those in the soil on Earth, additional fertilisers may be needed to grow crops.

CHAPTER 3
OUT OF THIS WORLD!

Most of the universe is too far away to visit, but scientists have been able to find out lots about it via some ingenious inventions. What's more, many of these innovations have been used to improve day-to-day life on Earth. Read on for the lowdown on probes, the Hubble Telescope and the mystery of dark matter...

MEGA MACHINES

Humans have sent special space robots to every planet, some moons, plus asteroids, comets and dwarf planets. Here are just a few of the spacebots out there right now...

LANDER

A spacecraft designed to land on a planet, moon, asteroid or comet.

ORBITER

A space probe designed to orbit a planet or moon.

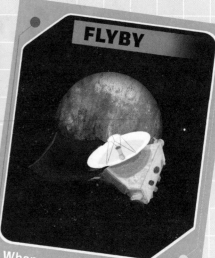

FLYBY

When a spacecraft flies past a planet or other body to gather information or speed.

Robots v people

Sending machines is a lot easier than sending people. The weight of the mission is lighter and so it's cheaper. Robots don't need food, water or oxygen and if the probe accidentally crashes, then nobody's hurt.

ROVER

A space vehicle that can travel on the ground of a planet or moon.

ROVERS have explored both the surface of the Moon and Mars.

VOYAGER 1 is the furthest probe from Earth – currently

23.8 BILLION KILOMETRES AWAY!

In 1966, the Soviet **VENERA 3** probe became the first human-made object to touch another planet's surface.

Ocean explorers

Jupiter's moon, Europa, is one of the most exciting places in the solar system to explore for signs of life because it's thought to host an ocean of liquid water.

ICY CRUST

OCEAN

MANTLE

The European Space Agency plans to launch the Jupiter Icy Moons Explorer (JUICE) in 2023 for a closer look.

Scientists are already talking about the possibility of sending the first machines out of the solar system to visit another star. A swarm of tiny computer chips could be fired there using laser beams beamed into space from the Earth's surface...

The journey would take a staggering 40 years!

SPACE SCIENCE

Loads of experiments have been carried out on the International Space Station (ISS) since people started occupying it in 2000. Here are just a few of the groundbreaking research projects undertaken in this zero-gravity environment...

Life in space
One of the main things scientists have been exploring is what being in space for a long time does to the body, mainly to see if humans will eventually be able to live in and travel around space!

NASA astronaut and Engineer Megan McArthur checks chilli plants growing on the ISS Columbus laboratory module ▼

Eat your greens!
While dehydrated astronaut food can work in the short term, it isn't stable enough to be stored in space for ages and gets nutritionally worse over time. NASA has now managed to grow eight types of leafy greens onboard the ISS, as well as radishes, to give astronauts a more varied diet.

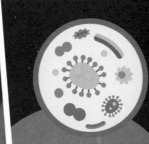

Medicine
Looking at cells without the influence of gravity gives scientists a better understanding of how to produce treatments for diseases such as cancer, asthma and heart disease.

▲
ISS crew members work together during an Integrated Immune Study blood sample draw at the Human Research Facility (HRF)

Salad harvest on the ISS

Green energy

Scientists discovered that fires burn differently in zero gravity as they use less fuel and are less polluting. Studying combustion in space is helping scientists understand more about fuels, which could result in more environmentally friendly ways of getting energy.

Turning wee into clean water

Efficient purification technology is needed to recycle the finite water supply onboard the ISS, as there aren't any rivers or lakes in space to get more from. That means it needs to be powerful enough to properly clean wastewater, such as astronaut pee! This tech can also help people back on Earth who don't have access to clean water.

COFFEE FROM RECYCLED WEE!

Forecasts

Due to their unique position looking over the Earth, astronauts can help forecast natural disasters and other weather events.

◀ NASA Astronaut Christina H Koch, looking through the ISS 'window to the world'

DOUBLE TROUBLE

In March 2015, NASA started a unique study with identical twins Scott and Mark Kelly. Scott was sent to the ISS for a year, while Mark stayed on Earth as a control to compare any changes to their bodies and health. They tested things like changes in genes expression, gut bacteria, immune response and brain speed. For Scott, most things stayed the same or bounced back to pre-test levels after landing on Earth, but some things, such as brain speed and accuracy, were lower on arrival and stayed at that new level for months.

Hooray For
HUBBLE

Floating 570 kilometres above you, the Hubble Space
Telescope has been gazing across galaxies for 30 years,
helping humans to understand the universe

ALL-SEEING EYE

Basic telescopes detect
basic visual images, but the
solar-powered Hubble Space
Telescope picks up ultraviolet
rays all the way to near-infrared.
Different sensors allow the
Hubble to show off space and
its stars in all their glory.

DISCOVERY DROP-OFF

The Hubble didn't blast off – it was
placed in space by the Discovery space
shuttle. On 24 April, 1990, Discovery
launched from the Kennedy Space
Center on mission number 35 of 39.

LIGHT YEARS AWAY

There's almost no limit to how far the Hubble Space
Telescope can see – so far, the furthest point is 13.4 billion
light years away! Galaxy GN-z11 is 134 nonillion kilometres
away... 134 followed by 54 zeroes!

SUPER SIGHT

The Hubble has made more than 1.5 million separate observations since it was set up! Its ability to peer into every corner of the cosmos is unmatched – with remote control, it can even track moving targets.

FARAWAY FIXERS

Scientists control every aspect of the telescope remotely. In 2021, the Hubble's computers stopped working, but NASA was able to fix a complicated payload computer issue and boot up backup systems, all from Earth!

HIGH TECH

The Hubble Space Telescope is still cutting edge when it comes to technology. Since it launched in 1990, five manned missions to the telescope have guaranteed that it continues to work at peak performance.

WHAT'S A LIGHT YEAR ANYWAY?

Space is so big, we need more than miles to measure it. Enter the light year – a measurement devised thanks to a genius maths equation!

Speed of light

Even light behaves differently in space's vacuum! Scientists know that it travels at 670,616,629 miles per hour. A light year is this fantastically far distance multiplied by a year on Earth – 8,766 hours!

670,616,629 miles x 8766 Earth hours = One light year (that's nearly 6 million million miles!)

Guiding light

Beyond 400 light years from Earth it gets hard for astronomers to measure the distance of stars in the sky. A star's brightness and the scope of its colour spectrum give us a good idea of where it sits in space.

Too far for now

How long does it take to travel a light year? Experts estimate about 37,000 Earth years! The furthest manned mission was 1.3 light-seconds – 240,000 miles to the Moon. Even that took three days.

I SPY...

FOMALHAUT B

Hubble observations have found faraway atmospheres beyond our Sun containing oxygen, carbon, hydrogen and water vapour. Scientists used it to take the first light-based photos of Fomalhaut b, an expanding dust cloud that was originally thought to be a massive planet... it lies beyond our solar system!

CRAB NEBULA

It's not just the birth of stars that Hubble has tracked... it's seen the death of them, too! The M1 Crab Nebula is what's left over after a stellar explosion. The gases it fired out helped to enrich brand-new galaxies in space.

FAST⚡FACTS

12,246kg – The weight of the Hubble Space Telescope here on Earth

27,350km/h – The speed the space telescope orbits the Earth. Try and keep up!

1990 – The year the Hubble Space Telescope was first deployed

EAGLE NEBULA

This cosmic claw-shaped gas cloud is the Eagle Nebula. Known as the Pillars of Creation, the tips of each 'tower' are forming gassy globules which will one day become stars! The tallest column is four light years tall!

ANDROMEDA

The largest Hubble Telescope image ever assembled is of the Andromeda galaxy, which is over 2.5 million light years away from Earth. Hubble is powerful enough to show us the individual stars in the galaxy – that's like taking a photo of a beach and being able to see each grain of sand!

INCREDIBLE INVENTIONS

Some of NASA's ideas are truly out of this world! And by solving problems in space, the space agency has helped to make your life easier, too...

INVENTION #1:
ARTIFICIAL LIMBS

Space problem: When your hands are full in space, important instruments have a habit of just... floating away! When their oxygen's ticking down, astronauts need total control over their experiments and their tools.

NASA's solution: NASA's best and brightest minds took inspiration from the natural world to make remote-controlled and robotic systems feel normal. They also made sure that they were as protected as possible.

HOW WE USE THEM TODAY:
Artificial limbs have never been better – or more high-tech. NASA's work enabling astronauts has not only improved on our capabilities but made these actions more comfortable.

NASA'S SCRATCH RESISTANT LENSES LAST **10X LONGER** THAN NORMAL GLASS

FAST

The first digital camera was designed in **1975** using NASA research

FACT

INVENTION #2:
SUPER SOAKERS

Space problem: No, really! In space, resources are incredibly limited due to space and weight restrictions. How do you power up tools without fuel for pistons and pneumatic machinery?

NASA's solution: A former US Air Force engineer thought about how pump-action pressure could power things in a way similar to a hand-powered bike pump. It was only a matter of time before he took aim at the weakest water pistols!

HOW WE USE THEM TODAY:
The Super Soaker is a great example of NASA's top tech-heads using their knowledge for FUN. Thanks to a build-up of water pressure, Super Soakers can fire up to 70 feet!

INVENTION #3:
DIGITAL CAMERA

Space problem: Lugging around an old school analogue camera isn't easy on Earth! Astronauts were finding that unless the camera was good to go on missions, it was all but impossible to prepare it in space.

NASA's solution: What if the photographs we took could exist on a computer? Today, it's normal! But NASA's work to transfer light into individual pixels on a screen was groundbreaking.

HOW WE USE THEM TODAY:
From drones and dashboard safety cams, to rugged GoPro action cams and smartphone sensors, digital cameras have changed the way we see – and interact with – the world around us.

INVENTION #4:
ENRICHED BABY FOOD AND FORMULA

Space problem: Houston, our astronauts are hungry! Even with next-level food prep, space travel can still leave astronauts without vital vitamins. Where do you find a healthy source of fatty acids that aid growth...?

NASA's solution: By researching the natural goodness in baby milk, NASA's scientists discovered they could make their own version of a fatty acid called omega-3 to keep astronauts in top condition.

HOW WE USE THEM TODAY:
These awesome acids have been used to boost baby formula back here on Earth. We can thank NASA for 90% of infant formula helping to develop babies' brains, eyes and hearts.

INVENTION #5:
NIKE AIR SNEAKERS

Space problem: From day one of spacesuit design, scientists' biggest challenge has been balancing comfort and survival. Even before we made it to space, firefighters were finding the same problems with their kit.

NASA's solution: Fire chiefs asked NASA to use the best bits of their spacesuits in a brand-new, safer fire fighting suit. 'Blow rubber moulding' lets designers line air pockets side by side to seriously cushion astronauts' landings.

HOW WE USE THEM TODAY:
Apart from making countless jobs much safer than before, NASA's super suit designs have made sports even more epic. When the engineer Frank Rudy pitched the idea to Nike, the Air sneaker was born.

INVENTION #6:
DUSTBUSTERS

Space problem: Ever tried to untangle a pair of headphones? Tangled wires are even more of a chore in space, so why not remove them? Much of a NASA technician's role is devoted to thinking about how to take out the friction in an astronauts' everyday tasks.

NASA's solution: During the Apollo era of space exploration, NASA teamed up with automatic tool makers Black & Decker to build a cordless sample collector!

HOW WE USE THEM TODAY:
From DIY projects to making medical procedures run smoothly, compact and cordless tools have changed the way we work. Next time you use a Dustbuster vacuum cleaner, pretend you're sucking up moon rocks!

INVENTION #7:
FREEZE-DRIED SNACKS

Space problem: The thing about fresh food is it grows (and was intended to be eaten) here on Earth. How do you preserve space food for years at a time without it being rotten by the time you get around to eating it?

NASA's solution: By sucking out the moisture in a vacuum, scientists made sure supplies stayed stable and didn't lose any nutrients along the way.

HOW WE USE THEM TODAY:
Just like in space, freeze-dried foods are great where foods might go off. Any type of food can be freeze-dried, making it healthier and smaller to store – why not try some freeze-dried fruit?

INVENTION #8:
EMERGENCY BLANKETS

Space problem: It's cold in space! Astronauts needed to avoid massive swings in body temperature to stay safe, and normal insulation materials were just too thick and heavy.

NASA's solution: The foil in space blankets reflects light and much more, and it protects the wearer from sudden spikes in temperature.

HOW WE USE THEM TODAY:
If you're going on a hiking adventure, you'll find a foil blanket like this in your emergency kit – if not, pick one up! You'll usually see marathon runners wrapped up in them after races and find them in sleeping bags, too.

INVENTION #9:
MEMORY FOAM

Space problem: What's the best way to keep pilots cushioned and supported as their bodies grapple with the high pressure of G-force while rocketing into space?

NASA's solution: Searching for ways to keep pilots safe and comfortable, scientists stripped away layer after layer of typical insulation and instead experimented with chemistry and moulding to make the most comfortable seats. It wasn't long before they invented memory foam.

HOW WE USE THEM TODAY:
While it's still used to keep space travellers safe, memory foam makes sleeping easier for people all over the planet. Not only does it soften a sore back, but it also moulds to reduce friction in artificial limbs.

INVENTION #10:
VELCRO

Space problem: In a spaceship, there's no right way up. From keeping dinner on the table to making sure pockets stay closed without fiddly fasteners, NASA needed a one-invention-fits-all solution.

NASA's solution: NASA might not have invented Velcro, but its use aboard Apollo 11 really put it on the map. It was used to keep so many things in place, one technician suggested they line the shuttle walls with it.

HOW WE USE THEM TODAY:
Can't tie your shoes yet? Don't worry! When it comes to backpacks, coats, shoelaces and pockets, Velcro makes making sure you're secure so much easier. Plus, it makes that very satisfying ripping sound!

INVENTION #11:
EAR THERMOMETERS

Space problem: NASA's Jet Propulsion Laboratory in California was looking for ways to measure the temperature of stars and planets for its missions.

NASA's solution: Stars and planets emit infrared radiation, and NASA scientists worked out that these readings could tell them the temperature too. Today's thermometers use the same technology – they determine your body temperature by measuring the energy emitted from your eardrum!

HOW WE USE THEM TODAY:
Rather than sticking a thermometer under your tongue, doctors are more likely to get an accurate, infrared reading from your ear.

Mars FEVER

Scientists have been looking for other signs of life in the universe for years, but it's Mars that has become known as the home planet of 'little green men' or aliens, also known as Martians

HOW DO ALIENS ORGANISE A PARTY?

THEY PLANET!

Frozen water on Mars

Looking for life

Today, covered with a layer of red dust, the planet Mars doesn't seem like somewhere that could support extraterrestrial life. Temperatures can drop to a freezing -140°C and its thin atmosphere cannot block ultraviolet radiation from space, which would wipe out anything living on its surface.

But scientists believe the planet was once much more like Earth, with a warmer climate and water filling its now-dry lakes and river beds. Of all the planets, Mars is the one thought most likely to have sustained life at some point in its very long history. Scientists hope that studying rocks, fossils and soil from the planet will reveal signs of living organisms – although these are more likely to be tiny life forms called microbes than little green men with flying saucers!

TEMPERATURES AS LOW AS -140°C

AB.C. 0123

TELEGRAM

The time received at this office is shown at the end of the message.

(PLEASE TURN OVER)

Office of Origin.   No. of Words.   Time of Lodgment.   No.

Office Date Stamp.

T.

C.

B.

HELLO, MARS

One of the first attempts to communicate with alien life on Mars was led by astronomer David Peck Todd in 1924, when he and inventor Charles Jenkins aimed a radio receiver into space, hoping to listen in to messages from the Red Planet. The search stepped up in 1960, when astronomer Frank Drake used a 25-metre diameter antenna in Green Bank, West Virginia, to hunt for signals that might be coming from two nearby star systems. Although Drake's antenna didn't hear any alien transmissions, his Project Ozma was a significant step in our journey to seek out and communicate with intelligent life beyond Earth.

Sch. A 0123-456789.

WOW, I'VE FOUND ALIEN LIFE!

Search for alien life

Today, the Search for Extraterrestrial Intelligence Institute (SETI) leads the quest for finding intelligent life in other star systems. Made up of scientists, engineers, technicians, teachers and support staff, SETI's Allen Telescope Array (ATA) at the Hat Creek Observatory in California is searching nearby systems for signs of intelligent civilisations. Further SETI experiments involve using large radio antennas to try and pick up radio signals transmitted by alien life.

Birth of the Martian

The idea of intelligent alien life on Mars all started with one mistaken word. In 1877, Italian astronomer Giovanni Schiaparelli reported he could see 'canali' – the Italian word for 'channels' – on the surface of the planet, which he was studying with powerful telescopes. When translated into English, 'canali' was incorrectly written as 'canals', leading people to believe that ancient canal-building lifeforms had been living on the planet: the legend of the Martian was born!

28221, Neg Em 34455

The Mystery of

The matter that we are made of, which we can see and touch, is only a small part of all the matter that exists in the universe. We don't know what the rest is! We call it dark matter

The ordinary matter that we know, called **BARYONIC MATTER**, is formed mainly of protons, neutrons and electrons. In contrast, **DARK MATTER** barely interacts with anything, not even light. The only way we can detect it is through the gravity that it generates, so it needs to have mass.

ORDINARY MATTER IS **ONLY 5%**

DARK ENERGY 68%

DARK MATTER 27%

WHAT DO WE KNOW ABOUT
DARK MATTER?

It does not interact at all with light – in other words, it does not absorb or emit photons, so we cannot see it. In fact, we could say that it is TRANSPARENT matter rather than dark matter

It has mass, so it interacts gravitationally

And that is all we know about dark matter...

It is neutral and has no electric charge

Dark matter is abundant and comprises approximately 27% of all mass and energy in the universe. To give you an idea of what that means, ordinary matter is just 5%! The remaining 68% is the even more mysterious DARK ENERGY.

In 1933, **Fritz Zwicky** (1898–1974) was the first person to suggest that dark matter might exist. Thanks to his observations of galaxy clusters, he realised that there must be invisible matter between the galaxies.

'95% OF THE UNIVERSE IS MISSING'
FRITZ ZWICKY

DARK MATTER

Trying to spot dark matter

We know that dark matter is everywhere, but so far there has been no sign of it. Scientists are trying to track it down and there have already been a number of scientific experiments to detect the 'particles' that form this strange matter.

It's thought that the particles that it's made of have very little mass, but it's so abundant in the cosmos that its gravitational effects are noticeable.

How do we know that it's there?

Although we cannot see dark matter, we can detect the gravitational effects of its mass.

For example, if we calculate a galaxy's mass based on its stars (ordinary matter), then we compare this with its real mass deduced from its gravitational effects, we'll find that 80% of the galaxy is missing!

A 'gravitational lens'

VERA RUBIN 1928-2016

Stars rotating at the same velocity in a galaxy

Vera Rubin was an American astronomer who found the clearest evidence of the existence of dark matter by studying how fast stars rotate in galaxies.

Stars that are further away from the centre of the galaxy should have a slower rotation speed. Rubin's observations showed that this was not the case. Instead, stars always rotated at the same speed no matter the distance from the centre of the galaxy. This can only be explained if there is much more matter around the galaxy than that which we can see: dark matter.

Another way to detect dark matter is through the gravitational lenses that appear in galaxy clusters. Light travels in a 'straight line' through space-time, but when it meets a massive object that deforms space-time, even though light has NO mass, it still follows the curved space and so its trajectory bends. We call this a **GRAVITATIONAL LENS**. If we were light, we wouldn't realise that we were travelling in a curved line, because all the physical space around us is distorting. Thanks to gravitational lenses we can see very distant objects that we wouldn't be able to see otherwise, because their light is too weak and because a massive body, like a galaxy or a black hole, is blocking our view. They're a handy tool for peering into the cosmos!

THE BIG
SPACE QUIZ

Read the issue, then put your newfound knowledge to the test!

1 How wide in diameter is the observable universe? (*Turn to p6 for a hint*)

2 How many asteroids have been found in the Asteroid Belt? (*Turn to p8 for a hint*)

3 What is the name for the dark blemishes on the Sun's surface? (*Turn to p13 for a hint*)

4 Why do we experience seasons on Earth? (*Turn to p19 for a hint*)

5 What is Olympus Mons on Mars? (*Turn to p21 for a hint*)

6 What is the name of the biggest storm on Jupiter? (*Turn to p22 for a hint*)

7 How many main rings does Neptune have? (*Turn to p25 for a hint*)

8 What did the ancient Romans call the Milky Way? (*Turn to p28 for a hint*)

9 What is the name of a cold cloud of gas and dust in interstellar space? (*Turn to p30 for a hint*)

10 What is the name for the boundary of a black hole? (*Turn to p36 for a hint*)

11 When did an asteroid wipe out the dinosaurs? (*Turn to p41 for a hint*)

12 What were the first animals in space? (*Turn to p45 for a hint*)

13 Who was the first person to go to the toilet on the Moon? (*Turn to p49 for a hint*)

14 Where did the Apollo 11 astronauts land on the Moon? (*Turn to p50 for a hint*)

15 How long do crew typically spend on board the ISS? (*Turn to p52 for a hint*)

16 How many astronauts have left Low-Earth Orbit? (*Turn to p54 for a hint*)

17 How far is Mars from Earth? (*Turn to p61 for a hint*)

18 What is the furthest probe from Earth? (*Turn to p77 for a hint*)

19 How many separate observations has the Hubble Space Telescope made? (*Turn to p81 for a hint*)

20 When was the Hubble Space Telescope first deployed? (*Turn to p82 for a hint*)

21 In what year was the first digital camera designed? (*Turn to p85 for a hint*)

22 What did NASA use to keep dinner on the table on Apollo 11? (*Turn to p87 for a hint*)

23 How low can the temperature drop on Mars? (*Turn to p88 for a hint*)

24 What percentage of the universe is made of dark matter? (*Turn to p90 for a hint*)

25 What is the name for ordinary matter? (*Turn to p90 for a hint*)

GLOSSARY

ASTRONOMER
Someone who studies space and the objects in it.

ATOM
A microscopic particle of matter, made from protons and neutrons surrounded by a cloud of electrons.

AXIS
The imaginary straight line around which a planet rotates.

CAPSULE
The part of a larger spacecraft that contains the crew.

CATACLYSMIC
A large-scale event that is sudden and violent.

COMET
A small, icy object that moves around the Sun, with a visible 'tail' of dust and gas particles.

CONSTELLATION
A group of stars in the sky that can be connected together into a recognisable pattern.

CRATER
A hole in the ground created by the impact of a meteorite.

DEHYDRATED
When a large amount of water is removed from food in order to preserve it.

DIAMETER
The length of a straight line from one point on a round object to a point on the opposite edge.

DRONE
A flying vehicle that doesn't have a pilot and can be controlled remotely.

EQUATOR
An imaginary line around the middle of the Earth or another planet, equally distant from both the North and South poles.

FERTILISER
A substance used to enrich soil so that it is easier to grow plants in it.

GALAXY
A massive group of millions or billions of stars held together by gravity.

GRAVITY
The force that draws objects towards the centre of a planet or star.

INTERSTELLAR
The place between stars or travelling between stars.

LUNAR
Related to the Moon.

METEOR
A piece of rock or similar matter from outer space that enters the Earth's atmosphere and burns brightly. Also known as a shooting star.

MICROBE
A microscopic organism.

MODULE
Part of a spacecraft that is self-contained and can be detached from the rest.

MOLTEN
When a substance has been turned into a liquid by heat.

NUTRIENTS
The substances in food that are needed to keep the body of a person or other living thing alive and healthy.

ORBIT
The path that an object takes around another object, such as a satellite travelling around a planet or a planet travelling around a star.

PARTICLES
The things inside an atom, such as electrons, neutrons and photons.

RADIATION
Energy or particles that come from something and travel across space, often in waves.

SENSOR
A device used to detect, measure and record the physical data in an environment, like temperature.

THERMOMETER
A device used to measure temperatures.

VACUUM
A space that contains no matter at all.

VENTILATION
The supply of fresh air to a room, vehicle, building or other enclosed space.

QUIZ ANSWERS

1. 93 billion light years
2. Nearly 1 million
3. Sunspots
4. Because Earth's axis is tilted
5. A volcano
6. The Great Red Spot
7. Five
8. Via Lactea
9. Nebula
10. Event horizon
11. 66 million years ago
12. Fruit flies
13. Buzz Aldrin
14. The Sea of Tranquility
15. Six months
16. 24
17. 225 million km
18. Voyager 1
19. More than 1.5 million
20. 1990
21. 1975
22. Velcro
23. -140°C
24. 27%
25. Baryonic matter

INDEX

First published 2023 by Button Books, an imprint of Guild of Master Craftsman Publications Ltd, Castle Place, 166 High Street, Lewes, East Sussex, BN7 1XU, UK. Copyright in the Work © GMC Publications Ltd, 2023. ISBN 978 1 78708 135 2. Distributed by Publishers Group West in the United States. All rights reserved. No part of this publication may be reproduced, stored in a retrieval system, or transmitted in any form or by any means without the prior permission of the publisher and copyright owner. While every effort has been made to obtain permission from the copyright holders for all material used in this book, the publishers will be pleased to hear from anyone who has not been appropriately acknowledged and to make the correction in future reprints. The publishers and authors can accept no legal responsibility for any consequences arising from the application of information, advice, or instructions given in this publication. A catalogue record for this book is available from the British Library. Editorial: Susie Duff, Nick Pierce, Lauren Jarvis, Jane Roe, Anne Guillot. Design: Jo Chapman, Tim Lambert. Publisher: Jonathan Grogan. Production: Jim Bulley. Photos/illustrations: Shutterstock.com, Rawpixel. com, NASA, Charlie Brandon-King, Eduard Altarriba, Alex Bailey. Colour origination by GMC Reprographics. Printed and bound in China.